T0196099

# Too Good
## to Be
# True?

# Too Good
## to Be
# True?

## ACCELERATED RESOLUTION THERAPY

*A Systematic Therapy Approach
That Changes Lives*

## Laney Rosenzweig, MS, LMFT

*Edited by Amy Shuman, MSW, LICSW, DCSW*

ARCHWAY
PUBLISHING

Copyright © 2021 Laney Rosenzweig, MS, LMFT.

All rights reserved. No part of this book may be used or reproduced by any means, graphic, electronic, or mechanical, including photocopying, recording, taping or by any information storage retrieval system without the written permission of the author except in the case of brief quotations embodied in critical articles and reviews.

Archway Publishing books may be ordered through booksellers or by contacting:

Archway Publishing
1663 Liberty Drive
Bloomington, IN 47403
www.archwaypublishing.com
844-669-3957

Because of the dynamic nature of the Internet, any web addresses or links contained in this book may have changed since publication and may no longer be valid. The views expressed in this work are solely those of the author and do not necessarily reflect the views of the publisher, and the publisher hereby disclaims any responsibility for them.

Any people depicted in stock imagery provided by Getty Images are models, and such images are being used for illustrative purposes only.
Certain stock imagery © Getty Images.

ISBN: 978-1-6657-0754-1 (sc)
ISBN: 978-1-6657-0752-7 (hc)
ISBN: 978-1-6657-0753-4 (e)

Library of Congress Control Number: 2021910816

Print information available on the last page.

Archway Publishing rev. date: 08/24/2022

*Dedicated to Judy Fryer*

*(From Left to right) The Dream Team: Robin Pickett, Multi-tasking Administrator; Amy Shuman, Lead Trainer and Laney Rosenzweig, Developer of Accelerated Resolution Therapy (ART); Judy Fryer, Head of Business Development and Founder of Rosenzweig Center for Rapid Recovery (RCRR)*

I needed a vehicle to spread Accelerated Resolution Therapy (ART). I was getting amazing results. Judy was my first cousin, a very favorite relative and an extremely successful businesswoman. She was like a mother and a sister to me. She was everyone's mother and loved by everybody.

Judy related to children so well, having raised four of her own and taking responsibility for others.

I approached Judy. "You need to make this a business. I am helping clients often in one session, and we need to spread it." She laughed it off until one day she created the Rosenzweig Center for Rapid Recovery. At the time, Judy and her husband Dick, founded and were running a successful real estate school, but Judy took the time to create The Rosenzweig Center for Rapid Recovery (RCRR).

As our cousin Brenda notes, "She made it happen."

When I ponder her secret for her admiration by others, I recall she listened and cared. Judy made you feel like you were the most important person in the world when you spoke with her and that your issues were her issues. She was always interested and asked many questions. Judy was the sharpest woman I've ever known. Even as she was approaching 84 years of age she was still answering our business emails right up to her death on August 31, 2021.

She was shy when it came to accepting compliments. A conversation with her would go like this:

"Look what you've done. Because of you so many people will get help due to the business you created to spread the therapy."

Judy's response was, "I didn't do it. It's your therapy."

"No", I would argue "My therapy would not be spreading without your business creation."

And so, we would go back and forth until we would finally agree we both played a part.

"Just remember I will always have your back," she would often say. I will always have her memory. She will always have a place in my heart.

## Acknowledgments

There are many people who have helped me in many ways over the years.

Thank you to ...
First of all, Judy Fryer, my dear cousin, who created and ran the business known as Rosenzweig Center for Rapid Recovery (RCRR), which has spread Accelerated Resolution Therapy (ART) throughout the United States and beyond.

Robin Pickett, who has been Judy's right-hand person for many years and now is also my right-hand person as the administrator for RCRR. I always say it would take three people to do her job; she is definitely a "multi, multi-tasker."

My lead trainer, Amy Shuman, who has edited the book with me. We have always worked well in concert together. I value the contributions she has made over the years.

Dr. Kevin Kip, who has been the first to research ART at the University of South Florida. He recognized the potential and the importance of the therapy enough to research whether it was, as he put it, "the real deal" and was willing to do the research.

Sue Girling, who has done a terrific job of running the International Society of Accelerated Resolution Therapy (IS-ART) and has had many supportive roles throughout the years.

Chris Sullivan, for creating a nonprofit organization, ART International, which was established to continue, along with RCRR, the spread of ART. I thank Pat Thompson and Kelly Bustin for heading up those endeavors.

Wendi Waits, who put trainings together for ART at both Fort Belvoir and Walter Reed. She was instrumental in introducing ART to the military.

Charles Hoge, MD, for sharing his clinical expertise in working with the military with me, encouraging pilot testing of ART, mentioning ART in his peer-reviewed publications on trauma-focused therapies, and facilitating a high quality head-to-head clinical trial of ART versus Cognitive Processing Therapy.

Olli Toukolehto, MD, board-certified psychiatrist, for his dedicated military service. He states, "Accelerated Resolution Therapy (ART) was my most utilized trauma-focused therapy during my nine-month deployment to Iraq. Most notably, ART allowed me to provide effective trauma-focused care for soldiers affected by acute stress reactions in operational areas that did not have dedicated behavioral health support. Single-session ART interventions proved to me exceedingly well-suited for the deployed military setting. I give ART my highest recommendation, and I hope that one day ART training will be available for all military behavioral health providers!"

Glenn Schiraldi, Ph.D., a renown expert on the Adverse Childhood Experiences (ACEs), first learned about Accelerated Resolution Therapy when reading studies about the "impressive and rapid results with the military." Glenn considers ART the treatment of choice for adult and childhood trauma because it is perhaps the most well-conceived and effective of the treatment options for trauma. We appreciate his support.

My family: Zachary Rosenzweig, who tells everyone about ART; and Joshua Rosenzweig and Priya Pathak, who have supported me and attended the ART conferences.

My brother, Arnold Zuboff, who kept at me to create the therapy so others could use it, my brother, Mark Zuboff, who recently passed, and cousin, Brenda Frank, for their unwavering support.

My deceased spouse, Alex Rosenzweig, who died at the young age of fifty-nine. I was so glad I could have an ART session to help me with the grief over my loss.

David Gordon, my current very significant other, who has also helped with editing and spreading the word about ART. I am happy he is in my life and is an extraordinary support.

The therapists who were in my first ART training and participated in the first study for ART, who took a leap of faith.

All the ART therapists and all the ART Trainers. I want to give a special shout-out to the Clinical ART Specialists: Amy Shuman, Colleen Clark, Mary Anders, Kathy Long and Marsha Mandel. They all continue to stay in touch on a regular basis as we move ART forward.

All the clients who have appreciated the benefits of the ART process. I receive numerous thank-yous, not just from my clients but other clients who have experienced transformations through ART. Thank you all.

**Laney Rosenzweig**, ART Developer

# Editor's Note

I rolled my eyes privately to myself. Laney and I were traveling together, in a crowded airport, trying to navigate the busy security line. I chose a different line that seemed to be going faster. I heard a little commotion to my left. It was Laney in the line next to me, it was her turn to go through the x-ray machine (that's what they were using in the early 2000s). Laney politely refused to go through the x-ray. She asked them, "Do you have proof that it doesn't hurt people? Do you know how it affects a passenger who travels often?" Of course, they didn't have answers. So she refused, and this was causing the little stir. Eventually they freed up a female Homeland Security agent who went over and gave Laney a body pat instead. Laney explained to me, "I just pretend I'm getting a massage." And it seems she was right about the x-ray machines; they don't use them anymore.

I like to tell this story because it captures so much about Laney. She is not afraid to do things the way she believes they should be done. She is polite. She is quite "outside the box," even eccentric. She is creative. She is persistent. I have told her many times that all of these qualities made it possible for her to think up Accelerated Resolution Therapy (ART) and to carry it forward for years, in spite of every obstacle, every closed door, every "no," every impossible attitude or question such as "What if they don't want to learn a new therapy?" And still she persevered, along with many talented therapists and other professionals who saw what she was doing and saw the immense value in it. We rolled up our sleeves and helped. It has been such a privilege, such an education to be one of those people.

Looking back, I find my journey with Laney and ART to be filled with deep learning lessons. We have been two curious clinicians, one with intuitive creativity and perseverance, the other with science and skills to hone and balance as we go along. This is an experience that can only come from a brave attempt to bring something profound into the unprepared world.

Laney, in her unconventional ways, used her practice wisdom, intuition, and perseverance to keep ART moving and growing. This left those whose job it is to respond, react, study, and decide in a quandary. The course that the reactions to ART takes is perhaps not unlike the paradigm shifts discussed by Thomas Kuhn, a renowned America philosopher of science, in his ground-breaking treatise, *The Structure of Scientific Revolutions* (2012). Kuhn takes us through the phases of reaction that we humans have to new scientific surprises. The ebbs and flows of understanding and then operation within each field follow this same course, and the landscape of human psychology, as soft a science as it is, is no exception. We, within our field, have had the surprises, reactions, and eventual settling that have been brought to us by Freud, Jung, Bowlby, Skinner, Perls, Rogers, Minuchin, Baker-Miller, and Shapiro, just to name a few. Each new paradigm, has gone through its phases and vetting process. Not unlike all other scientific fields, the field of human psychology follows the natural progressions and phases outlined by Kuhn.

The very idea is startling that instead of "therapy as usual," a client could choose not to talk about their problem and instead would be asked to move their eyes back and forth repeatedly while they replace negative images from memories with positive ones. And, if I dare say or even suggest that there could be a cure to PTSD symptoms, it is audacious. The fact that Laney used her practice wisdom and intuition, rather than following a deductive scientific course of theory, hypothesis, and testing, further compounds the incredulity of "reasoned professionals."

This dilemma calls for research, research, research. Research is needed at a time when funding for such research is nowhere to be found. And when a problem appears, so do the heroes. Kevin Kip has first and foremost, pioneered nearly all of the credible research to date. Philanthropist Chris Sullivan has funded, to the tune of one million-plus dollars, what we believe is the first privately funded research on the treatment of PTSD in the country, a study still continuing. We await the results of this head-to-head ART versus CPT "Gold Standard Study." There are those who will remain unmentioned who have dared to speak about a neophyte therapy in rooms where their message has not always been warmly welcomed.

And now, it has been just over ten years since I sat on Laney's carpeted living room floor, listening to audio tapes to learn how to do ART. The journey has not always been easy. There have been many surprises, disappointments, and successes. As a person who is skeptical to my core, I have been surprised and amazed over and over again as I witness my clients make profound shifts while engaging in a session of ART.

I have had the privilege to meet and work with gifted, dedicated people such as Kevin Kip, Wendi Waits, Charles Hoge,

Judy Fryer, Robin Pickett, Sue Girling, Diego Hernandez, Kathy Long, Vickie Alston, Maria Zygmont, Jo Shuman, and many, many more. We have all assembled ourselves around Laney and ART simply because ART works. And surprisingly, unexpectedly, I have made a deep and lasting friendship with this wonderful, exasperating, unique woman. It has been my honor to work alongside Laney and now act as midwife to her book.

May readers find possibilities in this book that they didn't know existed, and may scientific inquiry continue to add evidence, and therefore credibility, in order to further vet this amazing therapy that can help to heal the world.

**—Amy Shuman, Editor**
April 27, 2020

# A Brother's Perspective

In this book, Laney Rosenzweig will be recounting a large number of cases in which people have been helped with seemingly miraculous speed and effectiveness to recover from trauma and many other kinds of serious mental health problems, very often after having suffered for years. What helps them so powerfully is Accelerated Resolution Therapy (ART), a wonderful method of treatment developed by Laney.

Perhaps I should quickly make clear that I am not, apart from my peculiarly acquired knowledge about ART, an authority on mental health. I am a retired philosophy lecturer, formerly at University College London; and I am Laney Rosenzweig's brother. The latter is the reason that I know about ART.

In September 2008, my sister, who has long lived and practiced as a therapist in West Hartford, Connecticut, emailed me in London about the extraordinary results she had been getting with a new sort of therapy that she had discovered. She wrote:

'I have almost a perfect record of resolving a particular issue in one session. I cannot believe it myself. It is strange to watch people heal in front of my eyes…I hope I don't sound like I'm full of myself – I am as amazed as anyone else that this stuff works… No one is getting results in one session every time like me that I know of.'

What she had discovered was that putting together two well-established therapy methods, which had so far been for no good reason kept apart, unlocked the doors to the mind's own power to heal itself.

One of the two methods she combined was that of eye movement therapy. When a 'client' (what used to be called a 'patient') is following with his eyes certain sideways hand movements of the therapist, this strangely results not only in a calming effect but in rendering the thinking of the client both clearer and much more effective at bringing about deep beneficial changes in reactions to the things being thought of. (One of several theories attempting to explain this is that the looking from side to side, because each side of our vision is processed in a different hemisphere of the brain, brings about a greater meshing together of the activities of both hemispheres, which allows a rare degree of harmony between intellect and emotion.) The effectiveness of using these movements has been well researched and has been widely accepted, including by the National Health Service here in Britain.

The other of the two methods, the one that my sister combined with the eye movements, was to make the therapy 'directive' – it was the therapist's giving of active help to the client in developing thoughts that could heal. The eye movement method had first been used within a therapy tradition that instead prized a passive allowing of the client to free-associate, simply for the reason that the discoverer of the effectiveness of eye movements had happened to belong to that tradition. So, therapists trained in using eye movements by her had been warned against too much interfering with whatever might develop unassisted in the client's mind.

But clients left to themselves simply do not have the powerful healing tools of thought that are needed, in combination with the eye movements, to make the kind of great and rapid progress to the resolution of their problems that ART can bring. So, with the eye movements Laney combined some of the time honored techniques of gestalt, guided imagery, and the psychodynamic approach, among others. For example, using gestalt, Laney might actively develop with the client the thought of a scene in which the client meets and is reconciled with himself as a child. (Remember that the eye movements will increase the healing power of this meeting far beyond what it otherwise might have.) The client would not have thought of this without Laney's help – and neither would Laney have thought of it in any detail without the client's help; but together they would have turned the key and opened the door to a deep and lasting healing.

Laney has developed lots of types of ART 'interventions' like the one that I have just described: She has written, for the use of other ART therapists, a manual that is filled with such ways of helping clients.

What stands out particularly among these interventions, espe-cially in the treatment of trauma, are those involving 'voluntary memory (or image) replacement', in which the client, with guidance from the therapist, chooses a new positive mental image to replace a poisonous old one that had, perhaps long, been haunting him. The client, during eye movements, is then able to establish the healing replacement image so firmly in his mind that it can now be mercifully impossible even to summon up the harmful older image. Yet the client retains the memory as a narrative. It is only the painful image that has been replaced.

Problems that have been resolved by ART, for adults or children, within a few sessions – and often in one – have included post-traumatic stress disorder (PTSD), sexual abuse trauma, depression, anxiety, phobia, obsessive-compulsive disorder, addiction, grief, job or social relationship issues, chronic pain, tinnitus, stuttering, Tourette's syndrome, eating disorders and dyslexia.

My claim that ART works is by no means just theoretical or anecdotal. Research has shown with scientific rigor that ART works.

I know enough about ART to feel certain that any good-hearted, open-minded consideration of it must make one a well-wisher and supporter.

And now, at last, it will be my sister's turn to tell you about ART – something that she loves to do.

# Author's Note

Since the inception of Accelerated Resolution Therapy (ART), I wanted, and ART needed, a book. Through the joy of training therapists, and the amazement of my clients as they heal very quickly before my eyes, I knew one day I would share this in a book.

I am not a member of any organized religion, but I am spiritual, and I believe that a Higher Power has guided me through the creation of ART. I still question bad things that happen, and as I write this, I am homebound due to the coronavirus pandemic. Many have died, and many have my same fears of leaving home. I am sixty-eight and have Grave's disease. I never would have imagined, except in a nightmare, that going to the market to buy food, for example, would instill an unease in me, but it does.

I try, as my therapy does, to focus on the positives. Some of my positives are that I am able to focus on this book, and I am with my significant other, David, much of the time. To my knowledge, I have not contracted the virus. I have many struggles but not to the degree others may face, with a lack of basic necessities during these trying times. I am fortunate.

ART is an eye-movement therapy. I have learned through our research that eye movements are connected to a calming response in the brain. I have used them when I look away from the picture of the coronavirus shown every day on the news shows—that ugly red sphere surrounded by protruding spikes. The coronavirus images remind me of the newscasts that used to show the World Trade Center coming down again and again during 9/11. Since I believe that it is the images in our brain that cause the hyper-vigilance that can lead to anxiety or posttraumatic stress, I know that repeatedly showing these kinds of images is very damaging.

I tell parts of my life experiences in this book to give insight into how I created ART and the stories in my life that have molded me into who I am. I can be stubborn, but that stubborn attitude also helped me survive my depression as a child. I can be inquis-itive and question things others may simply accept. Growing up with a brother who became a philosophy lecturer, who questioned many things, definitely stirred my curiosity about life, and I often do not accept life at face value. I question.

The title of this book, *Too Good to Be True?*, was a natural choice, because that is what people say about the therapy's ability to get a client through a traumatic past event, often in one session. (As I always say, "Why suffer one more day than you need to?") ART is an evidence-based "eye-movement therapy" that some believe may allow access to the limbic system in our brains, which governs our emotional states. When we have entry into the emo-tional part of ourselves, it allows us, using the ART protocol, to make a deeper and speedier recovery from problems.

The fact that it is so good sometimes is a hindrance, because it can be easy to dismiss the therapy as a fraud. It is as if, some-times, one part of the brain, the cognitive part, can't quite make rational sense out of a sudden, gentle, but profound change in the emotional part.

I had also thought about calling the book *As if It Never Happened*, because clients often feel reset to the way they were before a trauma. My editor's opinion was that the result from the ART session is even better than if a traumatic event had never happened, and she preferred to keep our initial choice for the book title.

I could have called it *Freedom from Trauma* or *Erase the Trauma*, because that is what we observe happening with ART, but we settled on our original title, which we hear often: *Too Good to Be True?*

I liked the title *Too Good to Be True?* because that is what we so often hear when clinicians learn the therapy or clients experience the therapy. We are hoping that by reading this book, more people in need of relief from their mental health issues may give the therapy a try, and more clinicians may want to train.

I have been asked about the cover. Archway Publishing designed a cover with a hummingbird escaping from a cage. I gave them the idea of a bird, and when I saw the hummingbird, I said, "Humm!" Then I thought how perfect because hummingbirds don't belong in cages. It made sense to me.

One would think that something that was too good to be true might be spread throughout the world quite quickly. However, I think the Hula-Hoop got more traction than ART. In fact, because it is too good to be true, this has slowed down its progress to some degree.

The subtitle, "A systematic therapy approach that changes lives," was chosen because when therapists train in ART, they get specific scripts built upon a system that often has predictable results. ART is a creative procedure but is also following a scripted procedural guide, especially in what we call Basic ART.

There has been resistance to believing that, in an average of 3.67 sessions, the symptoms of posttraumatic stress can be eliminated, although the first randomized controlled study showed that participants experienced significant relief of their PTSD symptoms within that time frame. Indeed, I have worked with many clients who have only needed one session to resolve their trauma.

The fact that this is procedural in nature and not "talk therapy" means that the client does not have to tell the facts about their story. While doing this creative procedure, the client is the only one to view their images in their mind, and the therapist is a creative guide who uses the ART protocol to allow the client to make positive changes, which then elicit feelings that are more positive. Clients who experience ART one time for a particular problem often come back to resolve other issues, because they have evidence from the first session that ART quickly resolves emotional issues.

I would not have championed the therapy and trained therapists if it were not this good. I don't hold myself out as someone who is so charismatic that anyone would follow me off a cliff. It had to be real and effective, or I would not be training therapists in ART, using it with my clients, or writing this book. To experience the therapy is to know it is real, and to see someone you love having been healed thanks to ART is to know it is real. My wish is to let the world know there is a faster and more complete way to heal. When you erase negative images from view, with the therapy, you heal. It can be that simple.

I tell people, that after reading this book, you'll probably know too much about me, but as one clinician said, "It's your truth." And it is. Therapists who train in ART, and others, often ask how was this therapy developed, and here is the story, and more.

**Laney Rosenzweig**

## Introduction and Premise

### What Is Accelerated Resolution Therapy?

My story makes me who I am, and as the Developer of Accelerated Resolution Therapy (ART) I feel compelled to share it with you. In order to understand ART, it's helpful to understand me. I live, breathe and sleep this therapy. The characteristics that I have developed over my lifetime, and that are in my DNA, have influenced the therapy itself. As the Developer, I think that ART is one of the best trauma therapies in the world, as you will see, as I interweave my story with ART's story.

Historically, there are mental health therapies which incorporate eye movements (Hedstrom, 1991). I believe the "smooth pursuit" eye movements (smooth movement of the eyes back and forth) used in ART are powerful because they are calming and elicit positive changes in affect and perspectives, helpful in the healing process. In 2008, after learning about the power of eye movements, I incorporated them into my practice, which eventually became ART. Many of the clinicians that I have trained, and our clients, state how powerful the experience has been for them.

Memories change every time you think about them, and that is another element that makes ART work so well. This ability for the brain to loosen memories and open them up to the possibility of changes is called "memory reconsolidation." (Alberini & LeDoux, 2019). I knew nothing about this scientifically evidenced process when I brought ART to the world. It was just intuitive for me to suggest to clients that they change images that come up with memories that are troubling them.

When we engage in ART, we delete negative images (and associated sensations) from view and replace them at will with whatever we want. Because of the amazing process of the memory reconsolidation window, clients can choose to make images change, and the changes last. In effect, the client creates a new story that has new images that the client chose to replace the negative pictures they have been seeing. Clients can still pull up the facts but not the images.

We like to say that you "keep the knowledge and lose the pain." Clients report to us that these lasting changes cause them to feel better. They still can recall the facts of the event, but the troubling images (and associated sensations) as well as the internal and environmental triggers are gone. In my opinion, eliminating the images is the most thorough way to resolve trauma. Once you do that, the brain does not have an image to compare with other pictures. For example, if someone has a snake phobia, tree branches that may resemble snakes will now simply look like tree branches once you eliminate the negative snake images.

I am all about speed in getting tasks done and taking the path of least resistance. This characteristic shows in the therapy, working with clients to get them through their issues, often in one session per trauma, whenever possible. I don't like to leave things dangling.

If a client has a history of childhood abuse with several themes contained within, it may take more than one session. However, we have been able to have clients take "snippets" of their childhood and complete a session in one hour as they gain a distanced and less impactful perspective on their childhood.

I prefer to do ART face-to-face. At this writing however, the COVID-19 pandemic has caused many of us to work from home, affecting many people's mental health and the economy. *Social distancing* is a phrase that feels foreign as a request we need to adhere to. We are always talking about bringing people closer together, and now we are farther apart. My personal experience is a feeling of surrealism. I wake in the morning, just as I had after my mother's sudden death, questioning the reality of the situation.

ART is so powerful that I have advised clinicians not to do ART on tele-therapy or use any other mobile way of doing it unless someone is sitting with the client who is aware of the method of eye movements we use to keep the client safe and has agreed to be trained in Sensation Awareness Focused Technique (SAF-T) either before or at the beginning of the session. SAF-T is used throughout ART, and other professionals and parents are trained to use SAF-T for calming as needed.

Once the session has begun, the client spends a short time imagining the issue they are working on as a "scene." The first time imagining the scene can be very powerful and can bring up the negative sensations so they can be moved further on in the protocol. And as always with ART, the client does not have to speak about any of the content or can pick and choose what they want to share. That makes ART doable with any "assistant" willing to do it, with whom both the client and the assistant are comfortable.

Clinicians have been training in it because of word of mouth; as others they know and trust tell them about the results they have been getting. I developed Accelerated Resolution Therapy (ART) in 2008. I have trained thousands of licensed mental health practitioners in this model. Using ART, a traumatic event can often be resolved in one session so that the symptoms caused by posttraumatic stress are eliminated.

*Chapter One*

# TOO GOOD TO BE TRUE?

**A POSTAL WORKER IS** mauled by a dog. She undergoes three operations but remains afraid to go out of her house. After a single one-hour therapy session, she can deliver the mail again.

A physician dealing with COVID-19 is worried about developing PTSD and after one session feels she has the resources to endure her most important job, taking care of patients in the ICU.

A person presumed dead and left in a morgue, resolves that trauma in a 45 minute ART session.

A stroke victim has difficulty walking until, after a single therapy session, he can now walk a straight line.

A person traumatized by years of ridicule, diagnosed with dyslexia, can now read and understand a book after one therapy session.

A person wants to remember their past but cannot remember. In one session those memories start to resurface.

How is this possible?

The discovery of how to help people erase negative images from view in their brain, and the power of rescripting a traumatic scene from negative to neutral or positive in one's mind, is responsible for the therapy's success.

Some call the transformation magic. It is the magic and the science of our brain and how it can work when you apply the systematic therapy approach known as Accelerated Resolution Therapy or ART.

All you need to do the therapy is a therapy goal, be able to hold on to a thought (and if you are reading this, you can hold on to a thought), the ability to move your eyes back and forth, and the motivation to want to resolve an issue or problem.

I have witnessed ART solving all the aforementioned problems, and ART can do more, some we already know and some yet to be discovered.

*Chapter Two*

------

# THE THREE CRITERIA OF ART

**IF SOMEONE IS GOING** to be my client, I usually use ART exclusively. I take time on the phone with the potential client beforehand, listening carefully to develop an understanding about their need and explain how ART works. It is then up to the client to determine if ART is something they would like to try and for me to determine if they are an appropriate candidate for ART. I emphasize that they do not have to believe that it will work. Many of the clients who have made the most striking changes have been quite skeptical before the session.

Once that I determine that a client is an appropriate candidate for ART, I next want to determine three things:

- ✦ Can they move their eyes?
- ✦ Can they hold on to a thought?
- ✦ Are they motivated for change?

If a client has a "secondary gain"—that is, if there is a known or unknown motivation to not make changes—this could affect their success in meeting their goals in any therapy, and ART is no exception.

The improvement will come once the client comes to an understanding that moving to a healthier state will be better than the state that they are experiencing currently. ART is not mind control.

If a client does not want to make a change, they won't. The session is in the client's control the entire time. One case bears this out. A father brought his teenage son to me because of three issues. The boy was afraid of fire, he could not stay in his room alone, and he was sleeping in his parents' bed at night. The father wanted to remain in the session, and his son wanted that too. I explained that ART will work for those things, if his son is motivated to change. The father then put on headphones so his son would not believe he was listening. It's often best because we don't want to influence the client's thoughts with others in the room.

About three weeks after the session, the father called me. "I heard your voice in my head," he said. When I asked why, he stated, "He is not afraid of fire anymore, and he can stay in his room alone, but he is still sleeping in bed with me and my wife."

When the father asked his son, "Why are you still sleeping with me and mom?" the son replied, "Because that is your problem, not mine." This is a perfect example of motivation. The son's motivation was to not fear fire and to be able to stay in his room. However, he liked sleeping with his parents.

A client's secondary gain can be as simple as feeling dependent on continuing disability paychecks that provide for the family. Perhaps the client just wants to stay in therapy because it feels comfortable, as they like their clinician and don't want to lose them. They may fear facing the difficulty of leaving behind the predictability of continuing on as they have been. As a matter of fact, there is a protocol to help people who fear any kind of change that I call the *Fear* (fair) *Flip*.

One of the reasons I love ART therapy is that the onus of change is squarely on the client's shoulders, where it should be. Clinicians don't have to do the heavy lifting. This alleviates what we call compassion fatigue for the clinician. The clinician does not leave the therapy session with a burden but rather feels as light as the client.

Because this is a protocol, a creative procedure, it is not a therapy that puts the burden of initiating change on the clinician. Rather, the client does the work, coming up with their own perspectives and solutions, while the ART clinician is a creative guide. Their clinical skills and strengths are still needed. They need their clinical wisdom combined with their creativity in order to know when and how to use the creative interventions along with the set protocol.

We are often asked about dissociation and how it works with ART. I think dissociation has been very helpful to people who have been in situations that they feel are impossible. I remember when I was too short and too young to go on a roller coaster with my brother. When I reached the top of the roller coaster, I did not want to be there. So, I closed my eyes and saw myself opening presents on Chanukkah, and I was no longer "on the roller coaster." I had dissociated. My brother told me he had to hold his arm over me, or I would have fallen out. A fear of death contributes to Post Traumatic Stress. I lived with that childhood memory for years but now think fondly about how the dissociation was helpful. I believe that when clients are doing ART, there are moments when we all dissociate, especially when the client is engaged in *The Director,* creating their "good dream" in order to alleviate symptoms.

## More about the Development of ART

There is a cadence and a rhythm to ART. I have the client see parts of their scene, a bit at a time, and then use the eye movements to move those sensations each step of the way. Why not? I figured if it works, then I would have the client eliminate images and sensations as they went along. So that was what I did. I decided there should be a standardized amount of eye movements to create a rhythm and take away the guesswork of how many eye movements were needed.

The scientists and researchers are probably not happy with how I came to decisions about what to do (practice wisdom and intuition, and listening to my Higher Power), but since I felt there was a Higher Power in my life, I listened for that amount in my mind as I was first applying those eye movements to my new regimen. I "heard" a distinct number, which was higher than I consciously would have picked. I interpreted it even further to mean a hand movement back and forth as "one pass." That would be it. I tried it with my first client with amazing results.

ART was developed based on intuition combined with my knowledge of other therapies, and the creation of new interventions that are unique to the therapy. I know it is hard for some researchers to credit something as elusive, as resistant to precise description, as intuition, but ART, the fruit of my intuition, works. The proof is in the pudding, and I warmly invite researchers to put this pudding to the scientific test. My lead clinician said to me that when she was doing her postgraduate work, one of her professors talked about the pros and cons of achieving a Ph.D. She went on to say, "It was a good thing that I stayed at the master's level because she felt that getting a Ph.D. could have damaged my creativity and my ability to think outside the box." I do not believe that is true, but I also know that worthwhile contributions do not come only from clinicians and researchers who have Ph.D.'s.

Using this new procedure was giving me good results and a pattern to follow.

One day a woman came to my therapy room and discussed that she had a dream that an annoying little girl was tugging at her at the beach. She didn't know what it meant. She then said that she also always had an image of herself stuck at a window looking out, and she also never understood that.

As I began an eye-movement set with this client, I began to think back to graduate school. In this class we learned and practiced a Gestalt technique for one week. I volunteered to show the tape I had done to display my technique with a colleague. It was a short video. My fellow student had said that her mother was physically abusive. I told her, "Your mother is hitting your sister; go and stop it."

Quietly, in her demure way, she called, "Stop it."

I said, "No, you don't understand. She is really hurting her, pulling her hair. She's drawing blood. Your sister is in pain."

My colleague screamed, "Stop!" as loud as I imagined she could. There was silence. There was a broken tension. We laughed.

When we showed it to the class, the teacher said, "There are so many good things about this tape, I don't know where to begin." The class applauded, and one of the students yelled out, "She's better than Fritz Perls!" These are the kinds of moments we tend to remember. I felt strange. I thought it was average and did not expect that kind of reception. When I became a clinician, I declined to use Gestalt in my practice as I didn't want clients throwing pillows around or destroying my office.

Back to my set of eye movements with my client: I thought, *Here's my opportunity to revisit Gestalt.* The client saw herself at a window. "Go back to that earlier self and talk with her. See why she is at that window." I used the eye movements as she went back in her mind.

"She is mad at me," the client said and seemed surprised. Of course, I asked why. She said she didn't know, so I sent her back with another set of eye movements. She then stated, "Because I left her back there when we were abused!"

I said, "Well, go back and talk to her some more; figure it out with her."

After more eye-movement sets, the client reported, "She will forgive me if I forgive her, and we can be friends." My hair stood up on my arms. I had the chills, and I thought, *Wow*. Using Gestalt with the eye movements was going to work, and it was so interesting and so powerful.

I asked her at the end of the session to ask her "earlier self" what she needed. After a set of eye movements, she answered, "She wants to go to the beach with me." She realized that this image of the little girl at the window that had been intruding throughout her life was the same little girl that she had just now "met." The session had come full circle.

Several weeks later the client came back for a second session to report, "I usually have to be with people all the time. I am a singer, and after the performance sets are over, I seek people out. I found I didn't need to do that these last few weeks. I had my earlier self with me. We were okay. My husband said he has noticed a difference in me. He thinks I look more confident, and I am more relaxed."

The next ART development came when a client began recalling the deplorable way her father had abused her. It was sexual, physical, and emotional; she had it all. The episode she was recalling involved her dropping cereal on the floor as a five-year-old. Her father swept it up, dog and cat hair included, and put it in her dish. "Eat it," he demanded.

I told her to stop right there. I knew the Gestalt had worked, so I intuitively said, "You change it. You're the director; change that scene any way you want to." The client changed the scene so her father was the one who had the dog and cat–haired cereal in front of him to eat. The client laughed.

She also drove him to the hospital in her mind, at age six, and had him castrated. That brought on another laugh. "I've always wanted to do that," she exclaimed. "Why do I even think about him anymore? I am done with him." She added, "I can't see it the old way."

"I don't understand. What do you mean?" I asked.

"I can't see the old images anymore. I only see me driving him to the hospital." That fascinated me.

I wondered about how that would work with other clients, and I tried it again. It worked. That was the birth of the Voluntary Image Replacement (VIR). We now are very thorough with ART in the way we erase, paint, and replace negative images. We invite the client to add good images to replace the negative images.

Have you ever wanted to remember something but not written it down at night in bed? You wake up in the morning, and if you are lucky it is still there. I believe your brain, in cleaning itself out during REM, has done some erasing. Your item may have been included in the cleaning. Just this morning I remember thinking just before falling asleep, *I need to remember* … and when I awoke, who knows? It's forgotten. The REM eye movements, during the ART process, can erase negative images and replace them with positive images. I do not know if that is exactly the same process as what we do during REM, but I am so glad it works. It is the focal point of what we do: Erase and Replace.

I realized when working with clients that it wasn't necessarily the original image that they were upset about. The images could have changed over time through the imaginative process that we all engage in. The client could have added additional images that they created in their mind that were as distressing as the original images or even more distressing.

For example, there was a client whose best friend was shot to death by her boyfriend. She started out telling me about when they brought the body bags out. This was the worst of the troubling memory, and we started to work there. However, as we got into the session, she realized that indeed this was not the most troubling aspect of the memory, but rather it was what she imagined had happened to her friend when the boyfriend shot her to death. These images were emblazoned into her brain, but they were images that she created in her mind's eye when hearing the facts of the shooting, and it was those images that I needed to work with.

## Chapter Three

# GROWING UP

**I DON'T TAKE FULL** credit for ART, which drives some people crazy. A Higher Power has something to do with its success; the way everything fits together must come from somewhere beyond me.

My good friend and lead trainer, Amy Shuman, often says, "Laney, you were the one to bring ART into the world because of all of the distinctive qualities that make you, you!"

Looking back at my childhood, I am reminded that my family was neither the best of families nor the worst. Good or bad, we were unique. I grew up in a family that, from all outward appearances, seemed fine. However, when I think of my childhood, I frequently remember feeling isolated and depressed. I was never sure why. Others in the family may have different memories of what went on. Indeed, this had to do with the emotional distancing that was an underlying theme in my family.

Embarrassing moments I remember from childhood still have a sting. I took out a photo album from the past. Looking at a photograph of my younger self in a ballerina costume brought back the feelings of abandonment, embarrassment, and, for my earlier self, a horrifying moment. Now, I can take an adult view and feel compassion for my earlier self. As I have said, it is the images that cause the triggers, and this did.

The dance class was having a recital on stage at the Bushnell Theater in Hartford. I remember my parents dropping me off backstage and my wondering where they were headed and feeling frightened. My teacher arrived, and suddenly we were all pushed on stage. As I started to dance, my shoulder strap broke. I clenched my arm to my outfit and kept dancing. It felt mortifying. Somehow I made it through the recital and then felt lost again, not knowing where to go to meet my parents. It reminded me of the feeling I had when I lost my family at a beach resort.

I was about six years old. My family went to the beach. I twirled around a pole. Like magic it seemed that my family disappeared. I walked over to an elderly man sitting on a bench, who remarked, "What a cute little girl." I cried, "I'm lost!" Luckily, he took me to a food stand and reported me lost. I waited until my family strolled in to claim me, casually enjoying ice cream cones. This was one of those memories that added to my childhood insecurities since it stands out and is remembered vividly.

Our childhood memories are often responsible for our adult attitudes and contribute to our adult insecurities. These types of memories can lead one to be overprotective of their children, as in my case.

There is a scale to rate your childhood traumas. The Adverse Childhood Experiences (ACEs) are childhood traumas that can predict future medical problems. I believe ART's scripting of childhood trauma is helpful in both eliminating future mental health issues and physical health issues.

My parents did finally claim me, and I was relieved to head home. Although I don't have many memories of that time in my life, this one stands out, as I recall the family was eating ice cream cones.

This distance created strength in me as I learned that, in some ways, I was on my own. I was not physically beaten, although there were sexual innuendos and slaps on the butt from my father, creating a shameful feeling. On several occasions, he also slapped my teenage friends on the butt. Obviously, these friends avoided him whenever possible.

My father could be very detached but also had a kind side. For example, one day he brought home baby chicks, saying they were abandoned. Someone had brought them into the pharmacy that he owned.

When I was about nine, he brought home a runaway teen who had told him, crying in the pharmacy, that she had nowhere to go. I asked him, "Are we going to keep her too?" She did stay with us for a while until she became pregnant by someone she dated and left. I have no recollection whether my mother or father made any attempt to find her family; I'm guessing not, and obviously the police were never contacted. Those were very different times.

My mother was a schoolteacher and returned to graduate school to earn an MA at the age of fifty. She became a reading consultant in an inner-city middle school and loved her job. After she died, aged fifty-three, my father and brothers and I were invited to the school where she had taught. They asked us to give out an award named after her to a student who had shown the most progress in reading. Afterward, the head of the local branch of the NAACP came over to us. As my brother Arnold remembers him saying, "Gert was the only white woman that ever cared about our children." We also received a letter from the NAACP that described my mother as "color-blind."

Mom spent a large portion of her time gathering materials, often at her own expense, such as prizes for achievements, to help with her teaching. Her car was always filled with such things. I often wished for the kind of attention from her that she gave to her students. Many years later, my younger brother, Mark, expressed what I had felt when he said, "I think Mom liked her kids at her job more than us."

However, if my mother had not been there, and if it had been my father alone, it would have been disastrous for me. I sometimes grimly joke that I had a choice later: I could either become a psych ward patient for the rest of my life or I could become a clinician—and I like the food better on the outside! My mother provided some semblance of normalcy in my childhood, although I questioned whether she loved me. She expressed disappointment because she had always wanted a girl to shop with, and I didn't like to shop when I was younger. It's ironic that I now love to shop.

My mother was extremely creative and innovative. She developed a new and highly effective way to get students, who had been failed by the schools, reading—and loving it. She discovered that what primarily caused them to stumble was their reading of vowels. The pronunciation of these varied enormously while the pronunciation of consonants remained stable. She put together fun lessons on the rules governing how the sounds of vowels changed in contexts of different letters. She also made audiotapes that students could study at their own pace. This worked like magic. One student, who came to our house for extra help, exclaimed to her, "So this is what it's like to read!" I would hear those same words later when I created a protocol to treat trauma manifesting as dyslexia.

Before she died, she sent her lessons and tapes to a well-known publisher. The incomprehensible response we received from them was, "We already publish enough spelling books." Now that I have developed ART, and feel closer to my mother, I think of how both of us have pioneered new ways to help people overcome great problems. When the shootings occurred at Sandy Hook in Connecticut, at the time when my husband died, I still attempted to reach out and offer ART to that community. Their response reminded me of the response my mother had gotten. They said, "We already have too many therapists." I told them my therapy was different in the way it can erase negative images in order to facilitate healing more quickly. They repeated, "But we have too many therapists."

Since developing ART, I have come to realize that in much of my emotional thinking about my mother, I instinctively replaced the negative images with positive ones. Two weeks before my mother died, before leaving for vacation with my father, she came to me in our living room and hugged me. I will never forget that she said to me, "You are beautiful, and you are going to be a great success." This was strange; we had never before had a moment quite like that. I relive that scene whenever I think about my mother.

I did not even know what to say to her, so I said nothing, but I took it all in. It was almost as if she knew this was her last chance. I never saw her again. We had just started to move away from the usual anger that separates teens from adults as the teens grow into their independence. We had started to form a new relationship.

Even though she died while on vacation, I long carried the odd feeling that she would be coming home again, that it was just an extended vacation. Of course, my mind was protecting me from the pain. Many nights I would dream that I was with her. The reality of the eye movements during sleep made it feel very real. Every morning I would wake up and have to ask myself once again, "Is she really gone?" Even though I had this dream over and over, I did not have the ability to make changes in the dream to become reality, not until many years later when I developed ART.

I remember not crying at her funeral and wondering why. The tears would come later, mixed in with the confusion about my role in the family. I wondered if I was supposed to become a mother figure to my brothers, but that was not going to happen; they wanted nothing to do with such an arrangement. We all stood on our own and followed our independent paths, our norm.

One good thing was that everyone in my family would always say "Love you" at the end of any phone conversation and at night before going to bed. Although it could be argued that this was just a routine without real meaning, I felt that it did have some meaning and carried it into my later family life with my husband and children.

I frequently dreamed about abandonment. For example, in one dream, I was in a car being driven home from the supermarket, and no one was at the wheel. As I alluded to above, we can use ART to change dreams. If I had known about ART then, I would have put someone supportive behind that wheel. As an adult, I can still do ART and go back in my imagination and use what we call a "Gestalt intervention" (Brownell, 2010) to change the images of that dream of the past. I can now get the reassurance that I sought then.

My family attended an orthodox synagogue—not because of a passionate belief, but because an orthodox synagogue was at the end of our street. Convenience drove much of what my family decided to do. There is a positive side to this, and as I consider my childhood, I understand that the practice of finding the shorter route often plays a part in choices that I make as an adult, and most certainly in my development of ART.

I was the middle child and the only female child. My father was a bit old school. His chauvinistic ideas drove his enthusiasm for my going to college because that was how I would meet a man to marry. My mother, on the other hand, was a respected reading consultant and felt that higher education was the most important thing for a young woman to pursue. These contrary opinions were asserted all through my childhood and often left me feeling very confused and depressed.

As a child I often didn't understand why I was depressed. I had cousins who were envious of what we had. We lived in a nice house with a pool, a pool house, and even pinball machines in the basement. My father was a pharmacist, and his message was "You are what you do." I interpreted this as: "You need to be working hard if you want to matter." He was a workaholic, and in fact he installed a bed into the wall of his office area. Many years later, as he lay dying with dementia in a nursing home, one of the last things he said to me was "I was a pharmacist."

I wrote poems as a young child about feeling depressed. Finding my poetry, my mother remarked that she thought it was good enough to publish. That was the end of it. My poetry was a cry for help and was expressing my deep feelings of isolation. My mother was also depressed and may simply have viewed my feelings as normal.

Because of her depression, my pharmacist father would give her various medications. When I look back, I often think of the song "Mother's Little Helper" by the Rolling Stones, because back then people were not aware of how dangerous and addictive medication could be. Near the end of her life, my mother experienced highs and lows from the medications she was on.

The last few years of her life took on the usual pattern of addiction. I never knew if she was going to be very happy or angry and had to test the waters when I first approached her during the day. All in all, I think she did the best she could. She would sometimes indulge us. Though she was not the best cook, she would often phone us when she was about to leave work to ask what kind of food we would like her to bring us. I have to confess that this is not very different from what I did with my children; working long hours as a clinician, I had little time to cook.

I also would take my kids to a restaurant or fast-food place. My youngest son has said, "You are very good at taking us out to eat." I do have a few signature dishes of my own, but I'll admit I never enjoyed cooking. We do what we know.

Part of my depression was caused by my need to be heard. I often had to yell to be heard. One of the interventions that I use in ART frequently as the therapist, is to tell the client to imagine a megaphone in their mind while they are doing the eye movements, and allow themselves to scream through the megaphone whatever they need to say to give their sensations a powerful voice.

I have wrestled with the idea that we are inherently good regardless of what we do for a living. That is, we are human beings, not "human doings." Changing this belief has been a lifelong struggle. I remember even deciding to go to therapy because of this family-instilled belief, and I was out of work during my late twenties. Once I found employment, I had no need for therapy; I was working. I was important again, and I counted—according to the definition of self-value that I inherited from my father.

I also struggled through an eating disorder during my later teens. Attending a modeling class and being told I was five pounds overweight sent me on many unhealthy changes in lifestyle and eating habits until I became ill. My older brother, often touted by others as a genius and someone I admired all my life, "cured" me of my eating disorder. One day, home from school, lying in my bed weakened by my food restriction and nutritional depletion, my brother flung open my door and threw a book at me. It was Adelle Davis's _Let's Eat Right to Keep Fit;_ I read it, learned about nutrition, and realized what I was doing to my body. I now understood what I needed to do to get better. I never discussed this incident or my eating disorder with my brother following his "intervention."

I also developed an addiction in my teens. Once, when I was not feeling well enough to go to school due to my eating disorder, my mother took me to a doctor. The truth was that I had gained some weight and did not have clothes that fit. No one believed me, and they all thought it must be something more serious. The doctor did not inquire about why I was unhappy but did prescribe the tranquilizer, Valium. I would take the prescribed Valium, on and off, until adulthood.

One day, when I appeared upset, a boyfriend asked, "Why don't you just take a Valium?" Hearing this casual suggestion made me realize at last that I was addicted to the stuff—or at least that I was all too often using it as a crutch. I immediately quit cold turkey. There were times during withdrawal when I was squirming, trying to get out of my crawling skin. But finally, I detoxed myself.

During this phase of my life, my family did not sit down to eat together most nights, so my mother had no idea that I had an eating disorder. She was concerned after the doctor's visit and sent over my aunt, a nurse, to assess my condition. My aunt asked me, "Do you hear voices?"

I replied, "Yes, I hear your voice!" The family determined by consensus this was not a mental health problem. Following that year-long period of eating strangely I simply nursed myself back to health.

I took a class on eating disorders in graduate school. I decided to create a diary of someone with an eating disorder. I got in front of the class and read a week's worth of diary notes. I remember how completely boring it was to have an eating disorder. Monday my schedule was waking up and wondering what I would have for breakfast or wondering whether I would eat at all. Then I wondered how many calories I could eat at lunch, if any. My whole day was consumed with calories and the different foods that I would allow myself to eat. Then I would dream about food. Tuesday would look pretty much the same.

I read the daily-repeating schedule to the class. Each day that I read about sounded just like the day before. The obsession with food is what I know now every eating disorder has in common. Eating disorders are very stubborn and all-consuming. They also distort your thinking both because of the nutrition depletion and because of the nature of the disorder.

While taking another course about substance abuse to become a therapist, I noticed that I was in the right place. I earned an easy A for the course. The years I had spent in Al-Anon helped me understand the concepts we covered in this class. It seemed that I understood, even more than my peers, that the alcoholic's spouse needs to look at their part of the relationship. Many in the class said I was blaming the victim.

Al-Anon taught me, that if the nonalcoholic partner can look at their behavior and change it, making better decisions, then that will give the substance abuser or dependent person an opportunity to look at their own behavior. The nonalcoholic partner can stop the vicious cycle that perpetuates the dysfunctional patterns in the alcoholic marriage. Perhaps the partner will leave, or perhaps they will stay, but if they attend Al-Anon and look at their own behavior, then their life will be better, no doubt.

I often wondered, at least at the time I was in college for my master's degree in the nineties, why there was no course on the Twelve Steps. It is so helpful to have the knowledge and wisdom that comes from Twelve Step programs. I believe it put me ahead of the game, and using the lessons from the Twelve Steps in combination with ART can be very powerful.

For example, you can ask the client to choose the step that relates most closely to their issue and make the choice during an eye-movement set. When they use ART to make the choice, the step will connect more deeply on an emotional level via the limbic system. They are not merely paying lip service, while rotely stating the step, as people sometimes do. Rather, they are making a real connection to the deep meaning of the step.

I was raising my two children, working part-time, and going to school, eventually taking two courses per semester. I know that took something out of me, and I deeply admire anyone who manages to balance all those challenges.

As I said before, we were fairly detached in many ways as a family, including not eating together except for holidays. Living in my home often felt like living with roommates, not family.

Once my mother complained because I was not eating the steak she had cooked. She would always deliberately burn the steak so that it was completely charred because she was repelled by the thought that the juice was animal blood. I had tried my aunt's juicy, succulent steak and found I could no longer eat the charred meat my mother made.

My father took a steak I had been given and threw it to the floor. "Eat it!" he commanded me. I was puzzled for a moment, I thought, *How am I going to get out of this one?* I knew his anger was quick to pass, but I needed to do something in that moment. So I took a plate, put the steak on it, and said I would eat it in my room. I dumped the steak in the bottom drawer of my bureau, and after a half hour had passed, I brought the plate back to him. "You ate it bone and all?" he asked, and by this time he was laughing. I quietly agreed—and that was the end of it. Perhaps if my mother was able to use ART in regard to her meat phobia … who knows?

My younger brother was bright and, as we all are, very stubborn. One Father's Day, my father told us how he had witnessed many customers purchasing Father's Day cards in his pharmacy. I gave him one, but he focused on my younger brother, who did not. He demanded my brother sign a card my father had brought home. My brother signed it "Dick Van Dyke." My father was not happy but did laugh the next day.

A positive side of stubbornness is persistence. I use persistence to do what I know intuitively is the right thing for ART. For example, I was once asked to eliminate an intervention called the *Bonfire*, which is a metaphorical intervention that we use when we want to help the client eliminate entire themes of problems that have existed throughout their life. I was asked to make the change, because the concern was that the *Bonfire* would dredge up difficult-to-manage negative emotions. Truth be told, clinicians often tell me that they like that intervention, because clients often feel great relief after metaphorically getting rid of more difficult memories. I also love the *Bonfire* because of the look of relief and wonder on my client's face once they have completed that phase of the protocol.

I was a middle child, sandwiched between two very intelligent brothers, the younger had a congenital heart condition. When I was upset by my younger brother's teasing, I was told nothing could be done because of his heart condition, and I should just try to get along. We had differences as children, but as adults we became friends.

My older brother had been an only child for almost seven years and in those years received enormous amounts of attention and support. Before I was born, Fridays were referred to as Arnold's Day, when he would get special treats. I was a sensitive and often cranky child. My older brother explained that I disrupted the harmony of the household when I complained, wanting to have my needs met. He'd had nearly seven years without a sibling, enjoying a blissful life. I can easily understand, but had a hard time accepting his resentment of the change in the household because of a new sibling.

Although we have had longtime geographical distance between us and some discord in our relationship, my older brother has been extremely supportive since ART's inception. In fact, he has encouraged me to develop it further, as he very clearly recognized the implications of this therapy to help people heal.

Growing up with "middle child syndrome," I felt that I fell through a crack. I wanted to be heard but often felt inaudible. This caused me to cry out more or just isolate, going back and forth between those extremes.

I also had black-and-white thinking. I thought that people either totally liked me or didn't like me at all. And I liked them either totally or not at all. Situations were always either wholly good or wholly bad. Depending on the situation, I was either not as good as those around me, or I felt far superior to those around me. I would vacillate between those extremes, not often finding the perspective that shades of gray can reveal. Now I am well aware that I always need to search for the gray, and I often ask my clients to look for it as well.

When a clinician uses ART with a client, many of the interventions lead the client to change their perspective by seeing a problem from the other person's point of view while moving their eyes. The interventions suggest examining parts of themselves similar to those of others that seemed different, to discover that a problem often is not black or white.

I have used an intervention in which I ask a client to visit "Blackville, Whiteville, and Grayville." I ask them to spend time in "Grayville" and write a brochure that entices people from

Whiteville and Blackville to visit Grayville. One client said there were beautiful horses and beautiful landscape and scenery in Grayville. With the aid of the eye movements, she wrote a brochure enticing those from the other lands to visit Grayville. She said, "This is the best session I ever had!"

I was sometimes ridiculed in school because when I was in elementary school someone hit me in the nose with a basketball. I had a hook nose. It was often emotionally painful at an age when looks are important. In elementary school, I distinctly remember a student passing around a note with a drawing of my nose and seeing students read the note and hearing them laugh. The good memory from that experience was that I was sitting next to a very good friend and sharing a chocolate bar. I prefer that memory. This incident is a good example of one aspect of ART: replacing bad images (and other sensations) with good ones.

Prior to college, I was able to correct the medical and esthetic damage that had been done to my nose. Years after the cosmetic surgery, for some reason the cartilage moved, and I now have a pointed nose on one side. It's nice not to care. I feel sad for my earlier self. With the advent of ART, we can use the eye movements to go back and "rescue our earlier selves" out of those scenes. We become "The Director" of the memory, rewriting the scene, and the ART intervention can change the effect of what happened to us as children. The amygdala believes the new images and releases symptoms that were associated with the old images (or other sensations) (Kip et al., 2014). That is one of the reasons ART is so effective.

When a trauma occurs, the images and sensations skip the normal processing in the brain. The prefrontal cortex is skipped and not allowed to integrate what has happened properly. The images and sensations that accompany the recalling of the trauma go right to the limbic system, where we feel fear and other negative emotions.

In doing ART, my theory is that the brain has a chance to reassess what happened by opening the opportunity to do so with the eye movements. As the client imagines the trauma, the negative sensations and images are highlighted in the brain. Using the eye movements, the negative sensations and images can be removed from view with the methods used during ART therapy.

The ART process seems to turn off the alarm bells (in the limbic system) that may be overly cautionary and cause hypervigilance. Hypervigilance is not a safe condition. We want to be vigilant and careful but not overreactive. I usually use the metaphor "Don't shoot yourself in the foot" to describe the unhelpfulness of hypervigilance

The client can do what I call a "lucid dream" and create in their mind's eye a positive scenario whereby they can change the images to whatever positive images they choose with eye movements. This is what the researchers call "rescripting," and the sensations seem to change naturally and mirror the positive images.

*Chapter 4*

---

# THE JILLIAN CHRONICLES

**SEVERAL YEARS AFTER MY** mother's passing, my father left Connecticut to pursue his dream of living in Florida, something my mother never wanted to do. He also chose a partner who had severe emotional problems, most likely, I think, stemming from her father having left her mother when she was very young. To protect the guilty, we will call her Jillian, and he would refer to her as Jill. Since then, I have often thought I would write a piece called *The Jillian Chronicles*.

One of the first things that Jillian said to me was, "I had no father, and now you won't have one either!" She told me that my dad's bringing me items from his store was going to stop. She looked at any female as competition, including me. My father stayed with her throughout the rest of his life, first at our home and hers, then in Florida condominiums.

Jillian thrived on attention; negative attention was just as good as positive attention, and maybe better. As clinicians we should not diagnose anyone but our clients. However, throughout the years, I could not keep the words *borderline personality disorder, histrionic, alcoholic,* and *narcissistic personality* out of my mind when I thought about Jillian. I can still see her image clearly, as I find it fascinating (and no longer a problem for me), but this detachment took a long time because I did not yet have ART. She had flaming orange-red hair, was short and plump, and wore attention-seeking outfits. Several of her outfits were transparent, with mesh netting.

One of my aunts was traumatized by the feather outfit she wore sitting shiva (the Jewish ritual of the mourners greeting their comforters) for my maternal grandmother, who had detested her. My relatives could not tolerate her antics—though they were often astonished and sometimes even greatly amused by them. She casually attended the memorial gathering and had the audacity to be the first to approach the rabbi when he entered.

There was the time when she came with my father for my wedding. I took my father's arm as we walked toward a shop. Jillian jumped me from behind and bit my arm. My brother had to pull her off of me. At least that meant she would not attend the wedding. I told my father if she didn't come to the wedding, I would not call the police. I had been very fearful that she was going to create disturbances at the ceremony and the reception. The attack on me was her ticket out. The wedding became the only time I would ever see my father without her. My younger brother had a droll sense of humor. I guess I should have predicted he would comment, "She just stopped in to get a bite."

Then there was my oldest son's bar mitzvah. I received a call from the local hotel where my father and Jillian were staying. "You need to come and get your parents. She tried to use our lobby crisis, only for emergency line, for a local call, and when we asked her to stop, she made racial slurs. We are having an NAACP convention here. You need to come and get them before there is a disruption and they get hurt."

Off I went to gather them up. Jillian commented, "I did not get my continental breakfast." Rushing them out of their room, I said, "Move it or you'll be getting a bagel thrown at you."

I had a friend in the car with me at the time. I had prepared her for Jillian's attention-seeking methods the best that I could, and she said she was prepared for Jillian to say anything. Jillian opened the van door, took one look at her, and said, "I think I'll park my p——y right here." My friend's mouth fell open; she was not as prepared as she needed to be. Jillian had a great sense for the precise degree of sensationalism she needed to use to get the attention she craved. Every time I thought I had steeled myself against her attempts, she would do or say something to top herself and would win that attention—even if it only gave her a momentary thrill.

Once I went out to eat with my father and Jillian. I had never before seen anyone take an entire loaf of French bread and try to cram it into a purse. My father had described an earlier situation where he was stopped on his way out of a restaurant, and Jillian was asked by security to open her purse. My father told the restaurant manager that if he proceeded with the search and they could not find the silverware she was being accused of taking, he would sue them. They let her go. Continuing the story, my father reported that on the way home, Jillian asked him to pull to the side of the road, where she dumped the silverware into the woods. This was nondescript, regular restaurant silverware, and mind you, Jillian had unplugged her stove because she said she would never cook. My father was surprised as he really did not know she had taken it. I guess Jillian was fearful the silverware police would come looking for her, so she got rid of the evidence.

When you get enough distance from an event, you sometimes feel compassion for your earlier self. The postal worker who shared that she was mauled by a "vicious dog" said she had compassion for herself after becoming desensitized by her ART session. I feel compassion for my teenage earlier self who took on my brother's issue. He told me he could not stand to hear Jillian and my father having sex. He heard them through his bedroom wall. Since Jillian lived fifteen minutes away, I asked them to please go to her house, explaining my brother's issue. My father took a glass of Manischewitz wine out of her hand and poured it over my head.

As I recall the memory images, I can no longer feel the sticky liquid dripping down my face. At least they did go to her house. I feel compassion for my earlier self who endured that. Since this occurred many years ago, there has been time for this to desensitize. The distancing was natural, but I wish I had known about eye movements back then and how they can quickly put distance between us and the event(s) from our past.

On one of my visits to my father just before a hurricane, my friend and I were in a hotel. My father insisted we join him in his condo, which I questioned because of the hurricane and how high up his condo was. We were discussing this in a restaurant, and Jillian objected, of course, to our joining them, and we really were not too happy about it either. She was so upset at the thought that she left the restaurant, crossed the street outside, and stuck up her thumb. She was picked up by a truck driver, who I was told kept calling the condo for some time.

Later in the condo, Jillian's son called me on my cell phone. Jillian overheard as I begged her son to talk to her, knowing the consequences if he refused. Still, he did refuse. Jillian took a large ceramic bowl of fruit and flung it at me, yelling, "You are tearing me apart from my son!" My friend yelled a warning and saved me when I did not see that object coming at my head. I moved just in time. We ran to the condo lobby. My father chased us, begging us to come back. We did. We looked out the condo window at one of the motels on fire, adding to the tense atmosphere, and wondered if it was our motel. It was a sleepless night. I can still see the burning motel in my mind, but it doesn't cause me distress; therefore, no need for ART on this.

My father told me about the time Jillian had been taking pictures of Sammy Davis Jr. during his stage act. Sammy had motioned to her to keep taking pictures but she actually jumped onto the stage with him. I was told he said, "I'll give anyone a bottle of champagne who can get this woman off the stage."

One positive thing Jillian did was introduce me to the comedian Jackie Mason. When I was introduced, Mr. Mason said to me, "What do you do?"

I replied, "I'm pregnant."

He responded, "It's great work if you can get it!"

Jillian made such a fuss before takeoff on an airplane, trying to make sure that her needs would all be met, that some of the staff refused to fly. My father and Jillian were kicked off the plane. My father sued the airline and won a settlement. When I told my older brother that they had been thrown off the plane, he asked, "Was it in the air?' At least we could laugh about these situations at times.

At one point, my older brother informed me that he had over-heard Jillian saying she had hired a "hit man" to kill me. I had not spoken to Jillian or my father for a while. I did not know what was brewing in her head, but I took the threat seriously enough to call them and check it out. My father convinced me not to call the police and said there was nothing to it. As I look back, I think that I'd advise my earlier self to call the police anyway. I am just grateful that either she actually tried to hire someone but nothing came of it, or it was only one of her baseless threats to get more of the attention she constantly craved.

Once while I was visiting with a friend in Florida, while in the car going to an event, Jillian complained endlessly through the whole ride as my father drove. I was in the back seat with another friend, and when Jillian left the car, we asked him how he could possibly stand that. He pulled earplugs from his ears and showed them to us. We thought it was cruel punishment that we did not get a pair as well. When Jillian returned to the car, she saw them and said, "Oh, you've got those stupid things in again."

Jillian invited my brothers but not me to dinner. I think it's because I was a female. I told my brother, "You can't go; you need to defend me."

He responded, "But I'm hungry." I convinced him, and he got me invited. As I sat at the table and she placed a steak on my plate, I suddenly realized, *Wow, this steak could be poisoned.* As much as I wanted to be there before, I didn't want to be there now. I even fantasized about doing a switch of our steaks if I could cause a distraction.

For most of the many years they were together, Jillian would complain to my father and many others about his refusal to marry her. My father explained to me, "She isn't a nice person, but I owe her. She has been with me since I lost your mother." She attempted to marry my father near the end when he was in a nursing home with dementia, but the nursing staff blocked that due to his inability at that point to consent with an awareness of what he was doing. She took the last bit of money he had in his pockets and then told me she had no more use for him. "What good is he to me? You can have him now" were her exact words.

That was the end of their relationship, and I brought him to Connecticut to take care of him until his death. By this time, with his dementia, he referred to me as "ma'am" but occasionally did seem to have a sense of who I was. He would yell, "Help me," but I was powerless to do anything really substantial. It was terrible to see a parent deteriorate like that. I often wonder: if I had known ART at that time, could it have made new connections in his brain?

At the end of her life, when she was dying of cancer, Jillian would phone me out of sheer loneliness. "I don't feel well," she would say.

"I'm sorry," I would respond. She would ask me to be an advocate to get her caregiver to take her out for bagels. The caregiver was not allowed to do that and also did not have a car.

Jillian called me up when she was very close to death and said, "I don't think people like me." I can't remember how I responded, but I know I felt sad for her at that point. She was finally able to reflect back on her life. She had made her bed, and now she was dying in it. She had pushed everyone away, and now, at the end, she was faced with that fact. It's sad, but she had no time to change even if she could become capable of it.

Nobody volunteered to speak at her funeral, so I did the best I could when I was asked. "There has been no one like Jillian before, and there will never be anyone like her again. She kept my dad busy traveling, which he enjoyed, and I think I made peace with her at the end. Amen." That was the best I had and it had to be good enough.

All these images in my past are just interesting memories now. I've had many years to digest them all. They feel well processed to me. If ART had existed, and I'd used it in those years, I could have brought down my emotional temperature much earlier and handled things much better throughout my relationship with Jillian. My life would have been much more serene. Instead, I tried to figure out how to deal with her and my father, who was attached to her constantly. I tried to ignore them, to disengage. I tried to appease her. I tried to appease him. I tried to appeal to him. Nothing I tried made me feel any better. No matter how abusive our parents are, there is still this need to find approval and acceptance. The problem is, when we try to find acceptance from unhealthy people, it puts us in a bind.

Had I used ART, I think I would have employed another intervention called the *Intimidation Buster*. When using this intervention, we invite the client to imagine something in the scene that would remove their feelings of powerlessness. While moving my eyes, I would have dressed Jillian in an ostrich outfit in my mind, and that would have made me laugh and broken the tension. Jillian often wore feathers, and I could have turned her into an actual ostrich in my imagination, squawking and strutting and pecking. This would have caused laughter, and laughter breaks up trauma. I see laughter and comedy as the opposite of trauma.

I often wondered if Jillian's raucous and outrageous behavior during her overseas travels could add to the negative stereotyping of Americans. Indeed, everyone except my father were repelled by her behavior. On one occasion, my father and Jillian put their names on a list to attend Thanksgiving dinner at the Jewish Center. As a result, most of the attendees, if not all, crossed their names off the list. As I reflect back, I understand it, but I feel sadness about it for everyone involved, including my father and Jillian.

During my advanced ART trainings I share a script called the *Fear Flip* Script. I train clinicians to use this script to help a client get ready for change. Many clients are afraid of what change in their life would look like, especially when they have been living with something so long that they have accommodated to living this way.

During use of this intervention, while moving their eyes, the client faces their fear using the metaphor of a fair. Clients do not hesitate to go right into the fair, without consciously realizing it is a metaphor. Some clients tell me they feel as though this intervention has addressed their whole life. This script would have been something I also would have used in my twenties when I was dealing with Jillian. It would have given me a larger perspective and taken away some of the emotion and fear that I lived with.

*Chapter Five*

---

# EARLY ADULTHOOD

**MY MOTHER DIED AT** fifty-three, when I was twenty-one. She was far too young. My dad fell apart and was depressed for a long time. At night he would sit on his bed, listen to music, and cry. He was sad most of the time.

I very much felt that I was on my own. I was also very codependent, looking for my happiness outside myself and trying to please others. It was easier to focus on pleasing others in my dating relationships than it was to focus on my needs. I longed for others to complete me. The light inside me was not on unless it was shared with someone else, because I was an observer; I didn't matter as much as others did.

I remained that way for years until my cousin Judy, seeing that I was dating an alcoholic, told me I should join Al-Anon, the organization for people who are closely involved with alcoholics. Through the Al-Anon twelve-step program I learned about codependency, and I absorbed that knowledge like a sponge.

Eventually I sponsored others in that program, and it was then that I first thought I might make a good clinician. I learned what it was to focus on one's needs in a positive way. I learned that in my relationships with men, I had been enabling, running away from a healthy focus on myself and instead focusing on my partner, on fixing him—which, of course, never works and traps one in an endless cycle of ups and downs.

Alcoholics often have black-and-white thinking, which was familiar to me since that was also how I thought for years. The Al-Anon program taught me how to re-parent myself. Many of the insights I gained there factored into the ART interventions.

When I did return to school to become a marriage and family clinician, I could see that the academic world did not embrace the twelve-step program of Al-Anon. Yet clinicians, in my opinion, need to become educated in this, which could help clients reaching out for support. There are still no courses I know of that teach the twelve steps.

My father believed that if he provided a home and other comforts for the family, his responsibilities were completely fulfilled. After my mother died, he said as much. He cited all he had given us and said his job was done. Now he would move to Florida and enjoy the rest of his life.

From what he related, I'd say my father's childhood was not a pleasant one. The man who became his stepfather gave him a half brother who was the golden-haired boy. This stepfather made essential extra money by restoring peoples' old mirrors in his apartment. He would very carefully apply the expensive silver solution to the back of a customer's mirror and later, when this had dried, tilt the mirror up and look at the result. Once there was a flaw. My father laughed uncontrollably at the expression on his stepfather's face, and he was chased through the apartment to the bathroom, where he locked himself in. This story strongly suggests to me that my father's relationship with his stepfather was a difficult one, and that some of his stepfather's behavior toward him was what we now view as abuse.

After my mother died, my father began taking a series of paying boarders into our home. This brought on many roommate fiascos, each boarder even stranger than the last.

One of the boarders once ate a head of lettuce for dinner. Interesting, although I love salad, in my opinion, no amount of lettuce takes the place of one cracker, if you feel like a carbohydrate. This roommate was the tallest woman I'd ever met, and she began dating my younger brother's friend, the shortest man I ever met. They were mistaken for mother and son all the time.

Then there was a woman in her twenties who was rather unique. She kept telling me she wanted an orgy. I told her to stop saying that and dismissed her idea. One day I came home to find four men sitting on my couch and our roommate sitting on the floor with her pants unzipped while eating potato chips. I must have given them a very stern look, as one of the men said, "I don't think she is into this."

I told them, "Leave my house immediately, or I will call the police!" and I stepped outside onto the front lawn.

I pleaded with my father to get rid of her, to no avail—until she stopped paying rent. At that point I was told to call her parents and remove her. When they came, the troubled tenant was on the (landline) phone. She talked on the phone incessantly. Back then there were no cell phones, and I couldn't even get her to stay off of it when I was expecting a call from the Mayor as a part of my journalism job at the time. When her parents came, they had to physically remove her—phone and all, ripping it from the wall.

Later that night my older brother and I found bills from a neurosurgeon in the room she had occupied. In addition to those bills, there was a note that said that talk show host Johnny Carson had given her the right to kill my father because his feet were too big. We agreed that our father had asked her to leave in the nick of time.

Another housemate was a friend of my older brother whose parents felt that at the age of twenty-eight he should leave home. He did leave home and moved into our house, just a few miles away. He still went home for all his meals and to have his mother do his laundry. In fact, he spent a great deal of time at his old house but came to our house to sleep. Every night he would ask if I wanted to have sex with him, telling me how good he was and what I was missing. And every night I politely declined.

An older woman moved in who one day asked if I would like to accompany her to a massage parlor where she was going to apply for a job. I was writing for a local newspaper in Hartford at the time and thought I would go with her to gather material for a story. I felt sure that they soon suspected I was a reporter because I asked so many questions. In their cagey answers they managed subtly to imply that there were more ways for someone who worked there to make money than just giving massages. The housemate did not get the job, but I did write a story.

I loved another housemate who would disappear into her room each day and come out about forty-five minutes later looking completely refreshed and renewed. One day I asked her what that was about, and she explained that she did Transcendental Meditation. I wanted that peace too.

She took me to a place in Hartford where I could be initiated and given a mantra. I took off my shoes and went upstairs with a man who sat me in a chair with the smell of incense all around me. He told me the magic sounds I was to repeat over and over again. I never embraced the culture as my housemate did, but I did use the meditation technique for many years. I feel it added to my intuitive ability to take in what is around me and helped me put life together in a way that made sense to me. Yes, I was grateful for that housemate.

## Chapter Six

# MY EMPLOYMENT

**I ALWAYS WANTED TO** be a reporter. It seemed natural, as I was always an observer growing up, an outsider of sorts. I went to Hebrew school after my regular elementary school classes. One of the instructors said, "You are not acting out or bad, but you just sit there like a bump on a log!" That phrase stuck in my mind because I think it signified my observer status.

One of the clinicians who has trained in ART was a child sitting next to me when we were children in Hebrew school. As a "bump on a log" I disappeared so well that she suggested that once the teacher's back was turned, we go down the fire escape and go to the local store for a candy bar. We were in the back row. The window was open. When we returned, we waited for the teacher to turn her back to the class again and we slipped silently into our seats. We were never missed!

I always felt different, like an outsider. Even my last name, which started with *Zu*, put me at the end of the line. That helped me think, *If they turned the line around, I would be at the beginning.* That rarely happened; I was always the caboose and always an observer.

One of the most important things we do with ART is to observe. ART is a systematic approach because it has specific "scripts" that the therapist will follow. This is very different than talk therapy because ART's system often yields a more predicable outcome. It is creative because we can add interventions to the scripts.

Because the therapist is guiding the process while the client is doing the "work" in their own imagination, we don't have to hear details of the problem that they are working on. We do ask, "What do you care to share?" during certain points in the script; however, the client can choose not to share any of the details of their problem or issue. Because we are good guides and don't do the work for the client, we need to perfect our skills of observation. Every time the client reports their experience to us, we are ready to respond with the next guiding step.

Once I finished college, I had a temporary job doing secretarial work at a newspaper touted be the only one of its kind in the area, a black weekly paper. I asked the owner of the paper if I could write articles for free, and he agreed. I acquired a press pass and was able to meet several celebrities and get their autographs. I have a photo of me sitting backstage on a couch next to Tina Turner, and a photo with Muddy Waters. I also met Smokey Robinson. I enjoyed that part of the job, and eventually I even got paid for it!

Often my interviewees, especially the political ones, commented that I was "different." They said that unlike other reporters, I would quote them accurately. I often wondered if my unembellished articles were interesting. But I always returned to my belief that reality is just as interesting. I continued to pay close attention, observing and listening to their words in their entirety.

Another opportunity allowed me to write for a larger, well-known newspaper as a small-town correspondent. The main reporters were often impressed at the amount of material I found to write about. They had days with less news than I was able to produce. I found interesting angles on what others might have considered mundane.

I became very much an observer as a child. This may have led to my early desire to become a reporter. I enjoyed writing (and majored in English in college), and I enjoyed observing—a good match for that occupation.

In developing ART, we use almost everything we hear and observe from our clients to create interventions. For example, metaphorical phrases such as "My back is against the wall" are meaningful to us because these phrases seem to create an open invitation into the subconscious, and we can use that opportunity to gain entry with the eye movements.

We use ART's *Metaphorical Moment* intervention to have the client see a pictorial metaphor of that wall and then, using eye movements, move the stuck negative sensations. When they look again, it has changed on its own, much to the client's surprise. Next, while using the eye movements, the client intentionally changes that image, and the result is that they do not feel stuck anymore. They find their own solution by viewing the situation in a metaphorical way that translates into a real-life solution. I believe that when we imagine pictures such as that wall, the process of "imagining" makes the issue more accessible for change. "A picture is worth a thousand words," and the problem is incorporated in the image.

Once during training, a trainee talked about his twelve-year headache. I worked with him using the *Metaphorical Moment*. He turned his headache into a block of concrete. I find it interesting that he chose a block. It was immovable for the twelve years. Once the sensation was in the block, the sensations moved. He looked at the concrete again, and it now had holes in it, an opening in his block.

Then he changed it to the foundation of a house, and I asked him what it meant for his headache to be the foundation of the house. With the connective help of the eye movements he exclaimed, "I have to forgive." I used more eye movements, and he cried as he did the work in his mind to forgive whoever or whatever. His headache left, and the relief was foreign to him. I had him fill the space in his head with good images.

A teen felt that he needed to be perfect. After having a session where I used ART's *Metaphorical Moment* protocol he replied, "I don't need to be perfect; I just need to be wonderful, and I am." He further remarked, "I don't have to go beyond my limits, I just do the best I can." I told him I thought the best you can is perfect.

He cried with relief and said he felt free from the burden he had been carrying.

When teaching ART's trainees, I discuss my definition of the difference between perfect and wonderful. When you need to be perfect, you must keep doing things to be perfect. If you are wonderful that is a state of being, you just are, nothing to do.

After that session, I found a plaque at a store that states "You don't have to be perfect to be Amazing." Of course, I bought it and keep it in sight. It is a good reminder for us to recognize our inherent worth.

Sometimes a metaphor is manifested into a physical symptom, and with ART we don't need to know what the trauma is. The eye movements take care of the problem without our having to hear the content.

Here is another example: I was conducting a training in a clinician's practice. She spoke in whispers, making it apparent that something was wrong with her voice. She had been to several doctors who could not diagnose the cause of her lost voice. During a break in the training, I asked her if I could work with her. I then asked her to sing "Row, Row, Row Your Boat" out loud. "How did you know I am a fisherman?" she asked. I told her I didn't know that, my intuition had again kicked in, and she proceeded to sing. She sang quietly at first, and with the application of the eye movements I asked her to turn up the volume and gave her an imaginary dial. Her voice became louder and louder until it was a normal tone. When the other trainees came back into the room, they were puzzled because she was now speaking in a normal tone. I am always willing to try anything, and anything almost always works with the right suggestions and the eye movements. Her whispers were probably representative of her trauma, perhaps a metaphor for her.

When my kids were very little—my oldest was just over four, and my youngest was six months—both had colic, but the younger one was a severe case. I would run to the doctor, who put him on medication such as Mylicon. I put him in a swing every day at five in the afternoon, when it would start.

Looking back, I wonder what would have happened if I had the eye movements. I have used the eye movements on a baby about three months old who was tongue-tied and in pain. I tried moving my hand, but this baby would not follow. So I moved my whole body and she followed my body with her eyes. She became calm and started to nurse with her mother. When she was carried around, she kept looking to make eye contact with me again. She lurched her head back to see me. I did more eye movements with her. It seemed to calm her and to help her with the pain.

I decided to go to therapy when the children were small because I was juggling work and other life challenges. My therapist asked me, "What do you want to do?"

That was a puzzling question because my life was about my family and making them happy, I had not considered myself in that equation. I repeated several times that I did not understand the question. She continued to ask me, "What do you want to do in your life? What are your long-term goals?" I thought about it for about a half a minute and then said, "I think I want to do what you are doing. I think I would make a good counselor." I had been sponsoring people in my Al-Anon program so I thought this might be a good career fit. She said, "Then do it!"

However, I did not know if the timing was right as I was so busy with my colicky baby, a four-year-old child, my marriage, and my job. I thought I had to put me on the back burner. Giving it more thought, I decided that I would see what it would be like to enroll in a master's program for marriage and family therapy. I ordered a catalogue, and it looked interesting. I signed up for one class to test the waters. It was an introduction to substance abuse/dependence, taught by a woman who had worked clinically in the field for many years.

One of my assignments was to pretend I was First Lady Barbara Bush and create a substance abuse prevention educational program for school systems. My slogan was "High as a Kite on Life," and I created a T-shirt with that slogan on it. I received an A for the project.

After this was done, I decided to send my project to the White House. I wrote in the letter that I doubted that Barbara Bush would see it, but I thought I would send it anyway. One day, in the mail, was a big envelope from the White House. It was a letter signed by Barbara Bush in blue ink stating, "Your program sounds very good. I wish I had really thought of it." I called my professor and told her, and she exclaimed, "Holy sh——!"

Feeling confident, after that course, I took another class and found I had a knack for doing the masters level work with relative ease. I had found my niche. Taking one or two classes at time, it took over four years to complete my LMFT program.

I did an internship at a clinic in Connecticut where I would work for over two decades working for a variety of departments. I found working with the crisis unit and employee assistance programs was especially helpful in introducing me to trauma work; of course, most areas of therapy are inclusive of trauma work, in one way or another.

I often consider how important the counselor's question was in framing my life's mission. When we ask questions with eye movements during an ART session, it can be especially helpful to clients. It can aid a client in accessing and engaging more of their left and right brain hemispheres and bring clarity to their session. The clients may experience more life changing questions and answers as I did.

*Chapter Seven*

---

# DEVELOPING ART

**I ATTENDED AN EMDR** (Eye Movement, Desensitization and Reprocessing) Training, and I was struck by the idea of incorporating the eye movements into therapy, as there was a profound shift in my thinking during the eye-movement practicum. However, my experience was that we spent an inordinate amount of time positing theory, and I was thirsty for the application. To this day, by the way, nobody knows exactly what the mechanism is that makes the eye movements so effective. As a matter of fact, Francine Shapiro, the creator of EMDR encouraged research in order to ascertain the effect of eye movements. I am very grateful to Francine Shapiro for bringing eye movements into modern use in therapy techniques.

EMDR uses free association and bilateral stimulation to desensitize the trauma triggers. EMDR may be able to be done in one session, but I have met many clients who had previously engaged in weeks, months, or years of EMDR and were still symptomatic. For example, I treated a woman with ART who had been affected by 9/11. She had been desensitized enough to be able to pass by the 9/11 site after doing EMDR. Her subjective units of distress (SUDS), which measure the level of distress about a problem (Wolpe, 1969), had gone from a 10 (the highest level of distress) to a 4 after EMDR. She could still, however, "see" the body parts on the ground in her mind's eye. After our session of ART, she was able to go to a 0 (zero) on the SUDS scale, meaning "I can handle it," and she could no longer retrieve the mind's eye image of the body parts.

When I train EMDR clinicians in ART, I often hear my trainees say, "It (EMDR) is cumbersome," and "I get stuck." As my lead trainer, Amy Shuman, always says, and I agree, "We are standing on the shoulders of a giant, Francine Shapiro, the founder of EMDR, who began training clinicians in 1987." I appreciate that and am so grateful I did attend that training.

At the EMDR training, I bonded with the eye movements themselves. I did have a meaningful experience as it came to me that the eye movements would externalize a situation so that the person feels they are getting an unexpected answer—perhaps from their subconscious. What happened for me during my practicum at the EMDR training was that I had been angry at my mother throughout my life because she had put me on a bus for nursery school with all boys who were older. The bus driver was creepy. He may have been trying to help but still periodically stared at me. Who knows what that was about? I was terrified. I didn't know where I was going or what I would do when I got there.

I still do not remember how I got from the bus to the nursery school class.

What happened when eye movements were applied was that I naturally moved to an adult memory when I dropped off my younger son to daycare. His two hands were pressed up against the window, and so was his face as he was crying. I went home and called the daycare center and asked how he was doing. I told them if he was still that upset, I was coming back. I had only put him in there for two days each week to get the respite from his colic. So I called them, and they told me, "He is happy and looking at the fish tank with the other kids."

I connected this memory to a new thought: "Maybe my mother did something similar and checked on me too! How can I blame her for something I did with my own child?" That changed my perspective, and I appreciated that. I went home and told my son, home on a college break at that time, "I am so sorry I left you at daycare, but I called and you were okay; you were looking at the fish tank." He looked at me strangely and said, "Yeah, okay, no problem. What are we doing for dinner?" And that was it.

For my birthday, my youngest son bought me a card with a pin inside that said on it, "Survived damn near everything." Though I hadn't shared very much about my past with them, they could see some of the fallout as they were growing up. Once the trauma has faded over the years, with the passage of time, it no longer has a hold on me, but it took many years. When I think about my past now, it is because I choose to think about it, not because images are thrust into my mind (as trauma does) against my will.

Thinking of even the past pain now causes me no distress. It is a narrative. In my mind, I can apply any of a number of imaginative interventions in order to improve my emotional experience: "It is what it is." That's where I am about my past. It is what it is.

When doing ART, we have a client visually follow the therapist's hand as it glides smoothly back and forth. This causes the eyes to engage in "smooth-pursuit eye movements," which are found to be calming to the brain. The phrase "it is what it is" is one that I might use when they are working on acceptance.

I realized that the part within us that could be called our "earlier selves" holds on to the anger but lacks the adult view. Now as an adult I can use my adult wisdom to catalyze my reevaluation of the event. During the use of ART, we give clients the opportunity to evaluate past events and correct their earlier selves' views. With ART we are always "updating the computer," telling our subconscious, "It's okay, we are okay now, because those things from the past are no longer happening. They are just a bad dream."

I was sold on the eye movements and what they could do. I completed my EMDR training, already thinking, *I wonder if there is another way to use these eye movements without free associating. What if I put the eye movements right on the problem?*

During the EMDR training, after my insight about my son, I realized that without the eye movements, I would never have thought about or chosen to compare myself with my mother in the way I did. I realized the eye movements were not just calming but also made insightful connections possible. In fact, the problem was externalized, and I was able to reevaluate the situation from an objective point of view. I actually would never have wanted to compare myself to my mother in that way before.

I believe that the brain holds on to many things that we have heard or seen and can make a connection that surprises us. For example, I had a client who was torn between staying with his wife or leaving her for a girlfriend. I recognized him as a passive person, so I told him to go to his mailbox in his imagination, and a letter would be there that would tell him what to do. He "came back" after a set of eye movements and said, sounding shocked, "I don't like what the letter said." I asked him to share and he stated, "The letter said I should live on my own and get myself together before I make a decision."

At the end of the session, I asked how he liked it. He responded, "I didn't know I was so smart!" Perhaps he saw the advice that he received in his "letter" in a talk show or someplace else, and his brain may have retrieved and connected to it.

After my EMDR training, I used the eye movement for the first time with a client the EMDR way (free associative). I kept saying, "Go with that," after each time I guessed at how many eye movements to do.

The client said "Go with what?"

I said, "I think it is the last thing you just thought of." I felt incompetent. I wasn't sure what to do. Although I felt that session ended in a fairly good place for the client, I was not comfortable with not being sure how to use the therapy. I decided to follow through on my idea to try the eye movements right on the problem.

I find that free association can take a person off track and connect them to things that are only distantly related to a problem. Having a system and a defined script that guides you each step of the way is not only, in my opinion, more effective but also gives you a roadmap that has a beginning, middle, and end that can often be completed in one session. Changing the negative story to positive is not only possible but even necessary to guarantee that no triggers are left behind. Erasing negative images from view and replacing them with positive images (or other sensations) has a profound effect on healing.

I had an article about ART published in *The Hartford Courant*. At the time, I called the therapy Eye Movement Desensitization and Reprocessing (EMDR) because I thought, even with the changes I'd made, that was what I was doing. Then I met an EMDR supervisor who told me "I don't want to slap your hand too hard, but I don't know what you are doing. It is not EMDR. You either have to go back to doing it our way or call it something else."

In essence, my EMDR supervisor said I was being radical by not following their method. I had looked at Francine Shapiro's first book, the second edition of Eye Movement Desensitization and Reprocessing. On page 88, she wrote, "Refrain from viewing EMDR as a race to achieve treatment effects." I noticed we were very opposite in our views. I later wrote a paper on the differences between ART and EMDR that I give out on request.

I met Francine when she was meeting with a group of trainees. I was the first to approach her and told her how much I liked the therapy and how quickly it worked. In her book she had written she was not concerned with speed. I perceived her looking at me strangely after the comment. She was gracious to take a photo with me and sign good luck on an article from the local newspaper that was written when I thought I was doing EMDR.

With ART, I teach to be mindful to attempt to resolve the client's goal for the session as quickly as possible, often in one session for a particular "scene."

The amount of difference and the degree of differences between EMDR and what I would name ART surprised me. I seemed to disagree at every turn. It amazes me how she was able to have EMDR spread around the globe. She was an important figure who was able to begin the process of getting eye movements into the mainstream.

That was a long half hour ride home. I thought about it. My results were so good. Ironically, that supervisor took the ART training two years later. I told her that she was the one who told me I was not doing EMDR. She responded, "I hope I was nice to you!" I assured her that she was.

When something (an event or incident) occurs, if it is very important to you, you can recall it word for word. This is called a flashbulb memory (Diamond et al., 2007). I remember that moment when the EMDR supervisor told me I wasn't doing EMDR as an important crossroads in my life. I knew that the results that I was getting were fantastic and surprising when I did it my way. That was the impetus for me to begin thinking about creating the therapy we now know as ART.

My cousin Judy sent a copy of the *Hartford Courant* article about ART to her son, Dr. Kevin Kip. As a research scientist, Kevin had just received a government grant to study posttraumatic stress disorder (PTSD) at the University of South Florida (USF). He called me one snowy Sunday morning, introduced himself, and asked, "Do you want to come to the University of South Florida and lecture on your therapy? I'd like to learn more about it." I was surprised, as I did not even know that Judy had sent her son the article. He didn't have to ask twice, and off I went.

The talk at the University of South Florida came as a stark awakening. I thought it would be accepted and sought after immediately as I explained ART. There were some representatives of a VA facility present. I was prepared for questions about my therapy but not these types of questions. "What if our clinicians don't want to learn something new?" I was asked. How do you answer that one? I didn't. "What if you are the only one who can do it?" Was I some kind of anomaly? I didn't think so.

"I am training my first person shortly," I reported. "I'll let you how it goes."

One woman popped up out of her seat. "If she has something better, why don't we listen to her?" Ah, the voice of reason!

After the talk some interested attendees came over to thank me for the presentation. One of the VA representatives whispered in my ear, "I am not afraid of learning new things." And that was the first public appearance of ART.

Kevin and I are related through Judy. I hadn't met him, and I spelled his name incorrectly on the slides. He likes to refer to that. He included ART in his study, and the USF's Institutional Review Board (IRB) ruled that we were distant enough relatives that there was no conflict of interest, so the study would go forward.

Kevin received over two million dollars and included five therapies. The results of that study revealed that ART participants could complete treatment for PTSD in an average of 3.67 sessions. And Dr. Kip excluded my lead trainer and myself from his study. He wanted to show that newly trained clinicians could have meaningful results.

With ART, problems can often be resolved in one session. It depends on the number of "problem themes" a client has. And it takes an average of three scenes per theme for a client to work on multiple-incident traumas. Still, "a long time" in ART is consistently shorter than any other therapy that I know of.

My older brother and I had been estranged after my father's death. He was a philosophy lecturer at University College London, and we hadn't really kept in touch. I reached out to him to let him know what I was doing with the therapy. I thought he would be interested. His children had been having trouble falling asleep with a fear of the dark. I explained how I thought he should handle it using my method with the eye movements. I told him to have them make a better connection with the dark—fireworks, a birthday cake in the dark, whatever they wanted. I instructed him on the eye movements. He reported it worked in about twenty-five minutes per child, and their fear was gone.

He played an important part in this story because he pursued me for a month to "make it your own. It's really terrific. You must share this method with others." He repeated that throughout the month. He later reported that he concurred that this must be Higher Powered. It was not like him to pursue something this strongly, but he felt compelled to do so.

Once a reporter asked me, "What is the first thing you thought of after developing the ART therapy?"

"Don't get hit by a car before you pass it on!" I was seriously worried about that. I used to think about it in bed at night. What if I am not around to spread this wonderful therapy? What a loss for clinicians and clients. I became hypervigilant about taking care of myself more than usual, waiting for that first person to train.

I began writing. I had to go back and dissect what I was doing step by step. Every time I saw a client and used my therapy, the client would thank me. They rarely needed more than three sessions; and most only needed one if the problem that they were working on was a trauma from the past.

I sent a letter to the governor of Connecticut and enthusiastically told him what I had. I had no idea what would happen, but I was very excited. The governor gave the letter to the Department of Mental Health and Addiction Services (DMHAS) in Connecticut. The assistant director of DMHAS called me. "We can't afford to buy your therapy, but I am starting a private practice, and I would like to learn it." Every week she would come to my house. It was April. It was rainy. She had her umbrella at my door. She had a big, pleasant smile, and she reminded me of Mary Poppins. I would later tell her that. She was involved for many years. She would listen to audio tapes (the videos had not come along) and helped to usher ART into places where she worked or had connections. This led to more ART trainings.

One of the stories she liked to tell was about using ART with children who were afraid to go to the dentist. She described how they would manifest themselves into Superman or Superwoman, and their fears would be allayed.

People who develop new things often talk about starting "in the garage." My garage was my living room, and I trained the first few people there. We all listened to my session audiotapes, those I had permission to share. We relaxed in the living room, with me on the living room rug. They would smile with excited and almost confused expressions as they listened to the changes clients were making.

*Chapter Eight*

# HOW WE USE AMBIGUOUS WORDS, PHRASES, AND THE SUBCONSCIOUS

**I'VE PREVIOUSLY MENTIONED THAT** as the middle child in this unique family, I had many struggles. Needless to say, I felt as if I disappeared, as if I didn't count. As a child my bedroom was abutting a wall where I could hear the TV in the living room. I had the feeling that I was missing out. I have since learned of a new term: FOMO, "fear of missing out."

One of my favorite ART interventions with a client who is suffering from low self-esteem is to have them envision all their imagined earlier selves counting off. Each age counts in turn from the earliest to the present day—"one, two, three," etc., all the way to the client's current age. Then, playing off of the double meaning of the word, the ART clinician asks "Do you count?" The only correct answer is, "Yes!" This metaphorical intervention results in sensations of "counting" and this feeling of self-esteem transfers to the feeling that one matters. I use these kinds of metaphors and wordplay as an important element in ART (Rosenzweig, 2018).

*Wordplay*

A client came to me about a year ago with a baseball injury to the head. He had a lot of anxiety and feared he would never play again. He had problems with his hand. He had generalized anxiety from the incident. During the instructions for *The Director* (where the client decides how they want to make changes in the scene), I suggested, "Have a ball!" With the word *ball* here, I used a pun, pairing together his issues with the baseball and the positive connotation of having a good time. In doing this I believe that the subconscious replaced the negative sensation he had with "ball" in his incident; with the positive meaning of the phrase "Have a ball!"

I believe this wordplay keeps the subconscious engaged while we surprise the prefrontal cortex with the immediate confusion that arises, which seems to keep the communication channel with the subconscious clear. By getting rid of the scene, he was able to play again.

One year later, he had to do a deposition related to the incident. He came for another session, and his hand was numb after bringing up the incident and talking about it again. They had done a nerve test and found that the nerve was fine. His mother said, "Just send him back to that woman who fixed it the first time!"

He came in, and all I did was have him imagine rolling the sensations up in a ball and throwing it. I also did a *Metaphorical Moment* on a sensation in his stomach that wouldn't move. He changed it to a black hole, and I said, "Get rid of the 'whole' thing." I did one set of eye movements, and the stomachache went away.

When he looked back, he said, "That was really weird." He saw a roller coaster instead of the black hole (the client always has the last choice in what they want to do). Then I had him change it to a very special roller coaster. In this retelling, I am realizing that roller coasters "move forward," and perhaps this image represented his moving forward past this issue, which he left in the past.

Then I asked him, "How does this relate to your injury and how you feel?" He said something that I already had an intervention for. I call it a double-edged sword, with fear on one side and excitement on the other. I asked him what it meant, and he said, "I should just feel the excitement and not the anxiety." Anxiety and excitement are experienced similarly in the body; it's just our interpretation that gives it one meaning or the other. He left with no problem in his hand, no more numbness. We went to shake hands goodbye, and I asked if we could shake with the hand that was numb. I asked, "Could you feel that?" and he lit up and said, "Yes!"

As stated before, I realized that confusing the cognitive mind and keeping it busy as it ponders further, enhances our ability to access the subconscious and quickly move sensations when we use the eye movements. I had viewed a video of Milton Erikson. In this video Erikson stated to the client, "Last time you were here, you sat on my left."

The client replied "No, your right!"

Then Erikson replied, "Right!" This double meaning confuses the client and allows entrance into the subconscious. This is what gave me the idea to use wordplay in my therapy.

Unlike hypnotherapy, in an ART session, the client is consciously and subconsciously aware. After learning about Milton Erikson and learning about how hypnotherapy uses surprise to initiate access into the subconscious, I realized that there are many surprising moments with ART as well. Many hypnosis clinicians who have taken my training have pointed out that ART therapists don't have to do an induction in order to access the subconscious.

However, we do something akin to an instant induction. The element of surprise arises at the beginning of an ART session as use of the correct amount of eye movements shifts uncomfortable sensations very quickly, often leaving the client surprised. The element of surprise presents repeatedly through the ART session while trauma continues to fade. The client learns more about and gains insights into their problem through the use of the eye movements.

I had a client who had a fear of public speaking. In school, a nun had taken his arms and rested them on two stacks of books because he had been sweating. Having his arms in this position made his sweating evident, and this was very embarrassing in front of his classmates. When we did ART, he chose a director scene where the nun fell off of a stage while doing the cancan. I pointed out to him that his brain was telling him that he "could could" do the public speaking.

Another woman with a fear of public speaking had a stuck sensation. I asked her to put the sensation into an image. She turned the sensation into a boulder. "Yes, you do have to become bolder for your public speaking," I retorted with wordplay. The client laughed. I asked her to turn the boulder into whatever she wanted. "I turned it into a sandcastle," she said. My suggestion was to have her see people around her admire her sandcastle, watching and learning how to build their own. I suggested that if she was nervous to speak, she should think about her sandcastle. This client left with excited curiosity about her next speech for work.

Another client was working on a fear of flying. As I processed his sensations, he reported, "I feel grounded now." Our clients often come up with the best metaphors without even realizing it.

A client came to see me who was experiencing the effects of Lyme disease. I suggested that she visualize her husband giving her a lime drink to replace the word Lyme metaphorically. By the end of the session, she reported that her pain went away.

During one of my clinician trainings, I had some time left over. I asked the attendees to come up and offered them an opportunity to work on an issue quickly using wordplay. One of the clinicians had a "locked jaw" and had been unable to open her mouth fully for some time. She said she had tried everything including acupuncture, a laser treatment, and many other interventions. She came up to the front of the room. I used eye movements and said, "I am giving you a jawbreaker; chew on that!" After a minute or two of eye movements she was surprised and started touching her jaw remarking on how loose it felt. She was able to smile fully, and was extremely excited. Weeks later I checked in with her and her jaw was still loose. My theory is that the confusion that may have been caused by the phrase "I'm giving you a jawbreaker; chew on that!" may have kept her conscious brain busy while the subconscious handled the problem.

Another attendee had a problem with an uneven gait. I brought her up to the front of the room and asked myself how I could use wordplay to refer to her hip problem. As I did the eye movements, I simply said, "Get hip!" She was able to walk across the room with a steady gait. It looked and felt to her to be very even.

On the last day of the Enhanced training, we show videos of these trainees telling about the results they experienced.

*Chapter Nine*

# TREATING NAUSEA AND VOMITING

**HERE'S ANOTHER EXAMPLE OF** my use of metaphors. A woman with a vomiting phobia came to see me. This phobia developed after, as a child, she had vomited in front of her Girl Scout troop. In our ART session, I encouraged her to put her problem into a metaphor. This led to her imagining what drowning would be like. She then processed the feeling that she couldn't breathe using the eye movements. She then easily changed it to a scene that offered a solution.

Before the eye-movement set, she guessed consciously that she would pick swimming with dolphins. Instead, with the eye movements, her brain took her out of the water completely to jet skiing! I wonder if this was a metaphor for "rising above it" (an expression that my dad always used). By the end of this session, she was able to look at a picture of a woman vomiting that had earlier upset her, and now she had a very different reaction. With the lifting of her mood, she repeated over and over, "It's just a picture, it's just a picture," as she cried in relief.

Some clients don't recognize what their metaphor represents, but changing it still brings relief. One teen came with her mother to do ART in order for me to treat her vomit phobia. She suffered from this phobia for many years after her family was ill and vomiting. They said they had tried everything before coming to see me, which is often the case.

I asked her to "draw out the problem" (metaphorically) on my white board. I often tell a client that their drawing could be just a design, which I think appeals to the subconscious and makes it less realistic and more about the sensations. Prior to the ART session she went up to the board and drew a circle with red dots in it. After the session she drew a waterfall, probably not realizing that also represented vomit, but now it was a beautiful flowing liquid she could handle. Her mother was amazed that we could use the word *vomit* in front of her with no reaction—a word she normally could not tolerate hearing.

*Treating Eating Disorders, Nausea and Vomiting with ART*

Eating disorders are not as easy to treat as a vomit phobia. They have their origin in a core belief that this is the only way the client can gain control, which, of course, is a fallacy as it really represents a loss of control. I have trained clinicians at an eating disorder clinic who use ART and find it extremely helpful. It is an ongoing problem that may take several sessions to treat, although often fewer sessions than traditional therapy. People who have eating disorders, whether anorexia, bulimia, overeating, or eating strangely, all have a common thread which is obsessive thoughts about food and body image. It is the thinking patterns that are really the problem.

Body dysmorphic disorder, however, which often accompanies eating disorders, seems to lend itself to a more rapid shift. Asking clients to picture themselves looking at themselves in a mirror, while processing out negative sensations and focusing on the positives of their images, has worked well for me. They look surprised as their image does not appear to be distasteful, and they are able to stand there for some time looking at themselves.

Having personally experienced an eating disorder, I understand how someone can overly focus on their body and become an extremist with their eating patterns. Using the eye movements to correct one's view and perspective is very powerful. When I have a client focus on the positive aspects of their body and face, along with the use of the eye movements, their perspective often changes very quickly. I have them pretend in their mind that they are looking in a mirror and they process out negative sensations with eye movements. Then after they have practiced, I have them actually look in a mirror, and they see themselves differently. Some have posed in front of the mirror and look intensely and with a surprised look on their face, and state something like "I don't think I do look as bad as I thought!"

I've treated several clients, some children, with a fear of vomiting (emetophobia) with great results. In one case, the client went through her scene, seeing her earlier self as a very young child first exposed to someone sick, hearing her mother vomit in the bathroom. I suggested, "Perhaps your mother was pregnant?"

She exclaimed "Yes, that makes sense. It would have been the right time" (for her mother to be pregnant with her sibling). I asked her to go back in her mind and explain to her earlier self that her mother was pregnant. Giving the adult version, making sense to the part of her that was afraid and left behind, did the trick. She also explained to her earlier self that vomiting was helpful and the body's way of keeping her safe.

I did see a client with four years of nausea. She didn't know why and found it debilitating. She later said she had thought about suicide. Having had severe nausea when I was pregnant, I could understand how awful her life was. She had been to many doctors and, as she put it, every kind of therapy. She was wanting to try ART.

I used the *Metaphorical Moment* intervention with this client. She put her nausea into an image. It was a room where she was running back and forth quickly, nonstop. That made sense to me in accounting for the nausea. I checked in with her to ask, "Are you someone who is a caretaker, and do you put others first?" She said that was true.

She had been through many losses in her life. I intuitively felt she had the feeling she did not deserve to feel good. I had her, in her mind, go and get a "permission slip" from those around her now, and those who were deceased, to feel better. Her nausea began to subside. By the end of the session, she reported feeling 90 percent better, and the 10 percent was her fear that the benefits from the ART session would not last. Clients often voice that concern. This client was looking forward to eating without the nausea and left feeling more hope than she had felt in four years. I taught her how to use the eye movements for herself just to move any negative sensations.

In one demonstration during a training, one trainee said to me, "I'm not leaving here until you take care of my vomit phobia." By the end of the demonstration, she was able to look at someone vomiting in a video on a phone, something which earlier she could not tolerate. Now she was puzzling over the video and saying, "Show me something that is worse. She's too pretty for it to bother me." We pulled up another video, and once again it did not bother her. She then said she was now a "zero" on the SUDS measurement, pulling the indicator down from a 1, meaning "I can handle this now." Also, we noted that her need to find a less pretty person vomiting was a subtle indicator that the shift had already occurred in her brain.

Even the most profound changes that are witnessed by the clinician can be so subtle and natural to the client that the client may not even notice the shift unless it is directly pointed out to them. That is why, in addition to teaching self-use, the only homework that an ART clinician gives to their clients is to look out for any changes in their everyday life.

One client had the big fear that many have, a fear of public speaking. Like any phobia, it has its origins in earlier moments. This client would often gag before speaking, and sure enough as he went through his scene in his mind, he began making a gagging sound. I thought I needed to get a pail for him! With eye movements I said, "Quickly, put that sensation into an image. Go see what that gagging sensation looks like. Let the image float into your mind," I guided the client. "I see a slug," the client reported.

After he processed the connective negative sensations, I asked the client to look at the slug again. "The slug looks clear now," he said with surprise in his voice. "Now, change it to whatever you would rather see," I invited the client. "Now I changed it into an emerald stone." I asked him to see his future speech and asked him to "try to gag." "It's not there, I can't" he said, hauntingly with disbelief in his voice. "Are you curious to try it?" I asked. He answered in the affirmative and when a client is curious to try their phobic activity it has worked. He slides the prior 9 on the ART subjective unit of distress scale to 0. In his mind he envisions his earlier selves in the front row holding up emeralds, what a beautiful new connection.

"The RCRR team":

(Left to right) Robin Pickett, Amy Shuman, Me, Judy Fryer

Francine Shapiro was gracious in consenting to take a photo with me. She has influenced the most research completed on the psychological effects of bilateral stimulation and was the forerunner in bringing eye movements into the modern world.

THE WHITE HOUSE

March 29, 1990

Dear Ms. Rosenzweig,

Thank you for sending the drug program for
elementary schools which you developed for a
class assignment.  I greatly appreciate your
thoughtfulness.

With all best wishes,

Warmly,

Barbara Bush

Ms. Laney Rosenzweig
29 Linden Street
New Britain, Connecticut  06051

Your program sounds very
good. I wish I had really
thought of it.

LETTER FROM BARBARA BUSH DURING GRADUATE SCHOOL

HERE I AM INTERVIEWING MUDDY WATERS.

INTERVIEWING THE FIFTH DIMENSION,

MARILYN MCCOO IN FOREFRONT

INTERVIEWING TINA TURNER – OH MY!
WHAT DID MY PHOTOGRAPHER FRIEND DO?

MY SON, JOSH, AND HIS WIFE PRIYA.
NOW THERE IS A DOCTOR IN THE HOUSE.

My teenaged depression.

With my late husband Alex, who died too young.

My mother, Gert, who died when I was 21.

WITH MY PARTNER, DAVID.

My sons Zach and Josh.

My late younger brother, Mark.

With Josh.

Older Brother, Arnold, shows Father the
Nietzsche book chapter that he authored

SAME FRIEND WHO IS NOT A PHOTOGRAPHER.
HALF OF A BLURRY SMOKEY ROBINSON.

INTERVIEWING TAJ MAHAL.

My "nightmare costume" whose strap
broke on stage at the Bushnell!

WITH ZACH.

THE ZUBOFFS ON VACATION.

WITH MY BEST FRIEND AND LEAD TRAINER AMY SHUMAN IN
WASHINGTON DC 2014 WHILE TRAINING MILITARY CLINICIANS.

With Dick Gregory.

Coins awarded to Accelerated Resolution Therapy.
Top left from Ft. Benning, Top right from Ft. Belvoir.
Bottom left from Art International Golf Event.
Bottom right from Lone Survivor Foundation.

I took this picture of the 5th Dimension.

Another picture with Tina Turner.

## Chapter Ten

# CORE BELIEF

**THERE ARE TIMES WHEN** a person's core belief can be approached head-on. If you can think of an appropriate reframe choice, it can make a profound difference in our lives. A reframe can quickly change a perspective and challenge a long-held negative belief, to make a difference in someone's life. This can be even more profound when used with ART because ART can make very quick connections in the brain.

For example, during an ART training, a trainee expressed difficulty accepting positive acquisitions in his life. He said he felt embarrassed that he had just acquired a new car. He wasn't sure why but noticed that it was a problem he had when he received anything of value. He felt ashamed to enjoy it.

We used ART's "Scene Match", taking his sensations in thinking about his new car and matching them to the earliest time he remembered feeling that way. "I see a scene where I am walking out of a church with my family. Other kids are making fun of my nice clothes. I am feeling embarrassed. I am ashamed," the trainee reported.

My suggestion was "What if they envied your clothes, and your way of dressing set a good example for them? What if they are more successful in their lives in part because they felt motivated to get better clothes? They couldn't express their envy at that time, but it could have turned into motivation." After he completed the ART practicum during the training session, he drove me and another trainee to lunch in his beautiful new car. I said, "What a great car."

He answered quickly, with solid affirmation in his voice, "Thank you!" The trainee in the back seat gave me the okay sign.

*Chapter Eleven*

# GESTALT

**ART USES TECHNIQUES DERIVED** from Gestalt therapy, which was developed by Fritz Perls, Laura Perls, and Paul
Goodmann in the 1940s and 1950s. The best-known Gestalt
therapy technique is called "the empty chair." The client talks to
an empty chair, imagining that the person they need to confront
is there. In this way they can safely express their emotions. With
the aid of the eye movements, ART has clients go back in their
mind and do confrontations and express themselves with the
empowerment that the eye movements seem to catalyze.

I treated a client whose mother committed suicide when he was
twelve years old. He struggled with this, and I used ART's Gestalt
to have him visit his mother in his mind. He had thought that
he should have recognized that his mother was "too nice" during
that period of time, and that should have been a clue she would
attempt suicide again. When he went back in his mind to talk to

her—and with the clarity that the eye movements give—he was able to hear her say, "I am grateful you did not try to stop me. I would have done it eventually. I was so happy to be able to tell you I loved you."

Following that session, the client reported that he felt "set free" and now understood that the incident occurred just the way it was supposed to happen. I added that he might want to ask forgiveness from his twelve-year-old self, whom he had been blaming all these years. When he went back in his mind once again, his twelve-year-old said, "I will forgive you, but don't ever blame me again."

The client came for another session, and I could see that he had moved on, as he never mentioned the suicide again, but instead worked on a current relationship issue with his significant other.

The use of Gestalt applied with the eye movements is important to help externalize a problem. The client can go back and "update" their earlier self. They will bring their earlier self current, which will help turn off the alarm bells that have been stuck for years, causing the client to be hypervigilant. Clinicians know that being vigilant is being aware and safe, but being hypervigilant is unsafe. This is because hypervigilance arises out of "fight-flight-freeze" of the sympathetic nervous system, and vigilance arises out of the calmer parasympathetic nervous system.

When we train military clinicians, they often wonder about how service members sometimes believe that the hypervigilance will keep them safe. However, I believe that the better state of being is vigilance. When we do ART, we keep the lessons and the facts related to the memory; we just lose the hypervigilance and hyperarousal. It is much better to keep the lessons but lose the intense anxiety.

*Chapter Twelve*

———

# RESCRIPTING

**ONE OF THE AMAZING** things about ART is that I discovered that if a client changes the troubling images, this leads to a *natural* change of the formerly troubling sensations. Improving—or even *positizing* (a word I created because of ART)—the image, naturally eliminates the need for symptoms, because usually the symptoms are the person's attempt to cope with the troubling sensations.

Uncomfortable sensations include anxiety, stress, depression, emotional numbing, etc. Also, some uncomfortable sensations are purely physical, including pain. Often I think the "alarm bells" or the hypervigilance is the brain's way of protecting us from future events. Sometimes it is misguided and overprotects us with the symptoms. When clinicians engage a client in ART, the client sometimes chooses to "rewrite" the troubling scene to "It didn't happen." Doing so usually eliminates their symptoms.

Another choice a client can make is to battle the problem scene head-on and create a scenario where they are the victor instead of the victim.

A suggestion that I often give for the rescripting is to have the police arrive on the scene to arrest the perpetrator before the bad act is committed. Then I suggest they "positize" the scene, such as going out and enjoying themselves. As ART clinicians, we make as many creative suggestions as we can think of and also remind the client that they can make the scene so that "it just didn't happen." This way they understand their breadth of choice. They can make a choice that is in alignment with their own personal value system and unique culture.

Once I worked with a client who was sexually abused by a family member's friends. When it came time for her to make her change, I suggested that she create a "bubble" around her bedroom door and as the boys approached, they would hit the bubble with a "boing!" and fall away as cartoon characters. Following the eye-movement set, she laughed and said, "It is over!" There was the humor that broke up her trauma.

*Chapter Thirteen*

# CHILDHOOD AND MORE

**A CLIENT REMEMBERED SCENES** of sexual abuse from her childhood. Her earlier child began to cut, transferring the emotional pain to the physical where it could be bandaged. It gave temporary relief. In doing ART we went back to rescue her earlier self. "It is not you that is cutting," I told her, "It is your earlier self that wants attention and needs to be rescued." Once again ART would go on a rescue mission.

Gestalt combined with eye movements makes an excellent marriage for healing. The client was instructed to go back and speak to her earlier child. The earlier child, along with the client, would come up with an image that needed to be gone from view. Using ART's erase-and-replace, the image was gone. The client would ask her earlier self to come with her into the present to update her "computer" and realize the past is in the past.

Her jaw became tight, and I suspected that her father was probably assaulting her in her memory. We moved those sensations. "I had no one there to care for me when I was young." The father had abused her, and the mother turned away and didn't act to help her.

"You did have someone to take care of you, and that was you," I responded. "You are a survivor. You took care of all your 'earlier selves,' and you still do to this day. It is your strength that pulled you through, and it is that same caring that makes you such a wonderful mother to your son."

Here is a story that shows how ART can naturally externalize a problem involving obsessive-compulsive disorder (OCD). A client visualized his OCD, which involved his checking oil in his car every hour, as the devil. The part of himself that was helpful was envisioned as an angel. During his follow-up visit I asked how it was going. He explained, "My devil told me I had to check my oil while my angel told me I didn't. I let them argue it out and went into the kitchen to make a peanut butter and jelly sandwich." I love that story, and when I train clinicians in the ART therapy, I use it as an example of externalization.

I was asked to do a TEDx talk by an executive in a corporation that was sponsoring the local presentations. A TEDx talk is a showcase for speakers presenting great, well-formed ideas in eighteen minutes or less. A family member of his had been engaging in superficial cutting, and he told me that after the one session of ART with me, she improved so much she made the honor roll and had not cut again since that session.

In my TEDx talk, I referred to the woman, who, during an ART session, saw herself as a young girl at the window. This is the client who inspired me to create the addition of Gestalt to ART therapy. For the presentation for the TEDx talk, I did not present the fact that she had imagined that her earlier self had driven her dad to the hospital and had him castrated. I did not do so because the person who sponsored me thought it would be too off-putting. I changed it to her going to the 'parent(s) store' to pick out a new parent(s). The TEDx talk is still on the internet at this writing. The presentation can be found on the front page of my website, www.artworksnow.com.

I had a client with OCD. I used my therapy on him. He had ten compulsions. One of his compulsions involved turning the volume knob on a TV or radio to an even number, not odd. Three weeks later he came back. I took out my notes and inquired, "What is better since our last session?"

"I don't do any of them anymore!" he said.

"What do you mean?" I asked, confused.

"I don't do any of my OCDs anymore," he confided.

"Are you kidding me?" I asked. I did not feel very professional in asking that question, but I couldn't believe it—OCD gone in one session. Wow!

My cousin Judy Fryer and her husband Dick founded a very successful real estate school. She is the wisest businessperson I know. While in shock at the success of the session, I called her and said, "Cousin Judy, I think I am the best clinician in the world!"

"Why?" she asked.

"Because I was able to complete an OCD case in one hour," I replied.

"You probably are the best clinician in the world," she laughed.

"Then I need you to make this into a business because we have to spread it. Others need to learn this," I said. She laughed. She would continue to laugh about it for six months. She finally took it seriously.

I had chosen a name for the therapy by laying out possible words on my kitchen table. I knew the therapy was fast and it resolved things very quickly.

There was *Accelerated*; I picked it up. There was *Resolution*; I picked up that word. And it is a *Therapy*. That creates the acronym, A-R-T. My friend who was observing my word choices said, "They will confuse it with the traditional art therapy."

"No," I responded, "People will be able to distinguish it and know that they are talking about this therapy when they are talking about this ART," I felt confident people would recognize it. We do erase, paint, and replace images. It is art, just not put to paper but accomplished in our minds. (Although, I sometimes do use a whiteboard and have the client draw the problem before their session and their resolution after the session.)

Also, compared to other therapies, ART can be remarkably quick in the relief that it brings to clients. If a client has a history of childhood abuse with several themes contained within it, it may take more than one session. However, we have been able to have clients take snippets of their childhood and often resolve the issue in a session as they gain a distanced and less impactful perspective on their childhood. We can even have a person process their memories of an entire childhood in as little as one session.

The speed of change that some people experience when they do ART can be startling or even alarming. Sometimes we have to "process" the amazement that clients feel. ART clients and ART clinicians are not the only ones to be surprised by such a quick change.

I later learned about the *Nova* special film *Memory Hackers* (Strachan, 2016) and received permission to show the film in my clinical trainings. The film shows four different times when researchers say, more or less, "At first I couldn't believe it!" When I train, I speak about the exclamations!

The first was Nobel Prize recipient Dr. Eric Kandel, when he stated, "You are seeing a memory being formed right in front of your eyes!" (neuronal growth). Next was Dr. Kareem Nader when he and his rats demonstrated the power of memory reconsolidation. And Dr. Merel Kindt discovered that she could use the memory reconsolidation window and the medication propranolol to help people to overcome their spider phobia. She stated, "At first I did not believe it!"

Finally, Dr. Christine Denny did a study with mice who were manipulated so that they could move their awareness between a good memory or the present-moment uncomfortable reality with the flick of a switch. She did this using photosynthesis and light-reactive algae that were spliced into key neurons in the brain. When the light switch was turned on, the mouse remembered the "good place" with low light, bedding, and a nice place to hide. Then *click* and the memory was turned off, and the mouse instantly reacted to the stark and harshly lit surroundings that it was actually in. It demonstrated discomfort by freezing in the corner.

Denny shared, "I think the first time we did it, we didn't believe it, but when you see inside of the brains of these mice and to think you are only manipulating those cells and changing the behavioral output of the animal … that's science fiction!" The surprise that I felt matched the exclamations of these scientists when I discovered how ART worked with my clients!

When conducting the ART protocol with clients, we do what I call "Outprocessing" during a key phase. Outprocessing reminds me of what Dr. Denny did with the mice. While the reconsolidation window is open, the client erases the individual negative images from view and replaces them with positive images of their choice. When the client sees a negative image, they are upset, and this is often reflected in their demeanor.

Once they erase the image from view and replace it, their affect is lifted, and they describe feeling relief. By doing that, clients are more reassured that the improvements they have made will last and that the triggers may truly be gone.

I believe that it is the images (and sometimes other sensations) that cause the triggers and not the cognitions. For example, a woman who was diagnosed with schizophrenia was able to eliminate unwelcome auditory hallucinations. We had five ART sessions. In the second session she reported her voices were gone. I was happily amazed. The voices did not return, she said, during her other sessions when we were working on family issues.

I do not often get clients with schizophrenia in my private practice, but I'm hoping we can study that diagnosis further. I know with tinnitus the brain has been able to turn noises down and have a client focus on other sounds in the room, which the clients have found helpful. It appears to change the way the brain interprets sounds and what sounds it prioritizes and directs its focus to.

One client lived underneath an apartment where she could hear a tenant being murdered. She heard the screams and kept hearing them after the incident as she looked at her ceiling at night. "I think I have to move," she told me. We did an ART session, and I suggested she associate a different sound with her ceiling. "What about a song, maybe 'What a Wonderful World'?" I suggested.

"How did you know that's my favorite song?" she said.

"I don't know. You can put any sound you want to replace the screams you heard." She did choose "What a Wonderful World" and reported back she no longer felt the need to move.

More about positization: I made a positive connection between my thoughts about the core ingredients of ART and a movie I recently saw entitled *Once Upon a Time in Hollywood*. Although I don't particularly like to watch movies with violence, I was on a plane, and this was the highlighted movie. I decided to watch.

Skip the next paragraph if you don't want to have a spoiler to the movie.

There is a very negative episode in our history with the notorious Charles Manson. It ended badly with senseless violence. In the movie, a movie star, Sharon Tate's demise is rescripted. The movie's ending turned a negative into a more positive outcome. While there was some violence, this new ending gave me a better feeling. I knew it was not true factually, but the images I now have, again are more pleasing than the real story. I know the real facts, but the images and sounds are better, especially the very last invitation from Sharon Tate to Leonardo DiCaprio's character to visit her home.

This movie catches the essence of ART, which is replacing negative with positive, and I watched it play out in that movie. When a better thing happens in the mind's eye, then the better feeling comes, despite the fact it was not real. It is creating a "good dream" that can change feelings about an event and make it easier to move forward than when you think about the event, always remembering facts about what really happened. I sometimes explain to my clients that the past is a bad dream and not real in the present moment. We are going to create a good dream.

The results of Buck et al.'s grief study (2020) bear that out. I believe ART may simulate lucid dreaming in the client, which creates the opportunity to "fix" a problem by rescripting. This allows the brain to keep the facts but react to the "new dream" that has fixed the problem.

Buck et al.'s article published in the *American Journal of Hospice and Palliative Medicine* reported the results of an ART study targeting complicated grief in older adults who were caregivers for a dying loved one:

> To date, clear treatment guidelines do not exist for [complicated grief] and there remains a need for further evidence on brief, effective "complicated grief" treatments. The effects observed with ART in an average of just 4 treatment sessions are extremely promising. The significant changes in [complicated grief] and common comorbid conditions suggest that ART is an effective and less time-intensive alternative for older adults than currently provided by either [complicated grief] treatment or traditional hospice bereavement services.

Here is an example of how ART can change nightmares. I was headed to Florida to facilitate an ART training. My business administrator, Robin, told me that she had arranged for a news crew to do a story on ART. I inquired what client we would ask to be featured in the news story. "I've arranged for you to see someone the day before the news crew comes," she explained. She also explained the client had a brain injury. It was a bit of pressure. I trusted ART but was not sure how this would go. Robin knew that a client needed to be able to hold on to a thought, be able to comfortably move their eyes, and be motivated for change, so I would just have to trust this would work out well for the client and the news crew.

The client described her issue. She and her spouse had been detectives. Her husband had hit her in the head with a gun. She was foggy but not knocked out by the blow. He was intending that the blow would kill her but it didn't. Instead, she recognized what he was trying to do and did some fast thinking to get him away. She said to him, "I need a baking pan; go get one from our neighbor." After he left the house, she heard a gunshot. She walked out and found him dead, by a self-inflicted gunshot wound.

She dreamed every night for years that he was coming back to get her. Her nightmares overwhelmed her. She chose to process this trauma using ART. She reported feeling relief at the conclusion of the session.

The next morning, she came in before the news crew arrived. "How are you doing?" I asked. "Have you noticed any changes since yesterday?" I wondered what could have changed since yesterday and hoped that her relief had lasted.

"The dream," she began. "The dream changed." She explained that she had dreamed every single night since the incident that he was still going to try to kill her. "Last night, after our session, I dreamed that he and I were on his boat, and he told me, 'I am sorry that I tried to kill you; I will never try that again,' and that was relief!"

The news crew came in. She had brought in pictures of her wedding and other photos that held much better memories for her. The photos appeared in the news spot as she explained her dream had changed from one that instilled terror in her to one that now made her feel peace with the past and hopeful for the future. I was very happy for her.

This story was an example of how a dream naturally shifted after an ART session. We can also use a dream as the targeted memory to change in an ART session. We use the dream as the "scene" and follow the usual ART protocol. In my experience this has worked remarkably well. The client usually reports that they don't have the dream anymore.

*Chapter Fourteen*

# ART AND THE MILITARY

**CHRIS SULLIVAN, A RESTAURATEUR,** and one of the founders of Outback Steakhouse, Bonefish Grill, and many other restaurants, had donated money to USF. Once he learned about ART, he became a vital benefactor. I met him once at one of his restaurants. He has been committed to spreading the therapy, as he has seen the effective results of ART and knows how it has helped others especially our war veterans. He founded ART International, a nonprofit organization, in order to further the spread of ART.

Kevin Kip introduced me to a veteran who had served in the military. That man arranged for me to talk about ART at a well-respected military hospital. Several of us gave our introduction to ART. A Green Beret veteran who had severe PTSD had been through three courses of prolonged exposure therapy but was still symptomatic. Prolonged exposure therapy is a comparatively long-term therapy in which the client learns to gradually approach the traumatic material by revisiting it repeatedly. I had been asked to do a session on him at USF. He only had that one session, and he no longer experienced symptoms. He later reported, "It saved my life."

We did not know how involved he would become. He founded The Veterans Alternative now named Warrior Wellness. ART is central to the program, which is free to veterans.

I think back to the day that the Green Beret came for his ART session. He said he had heard about the therapy and wanted five sessions before I traveled back home. I said, "Try one," and he did. I did not hear any of the details of what happened to him until many years later.

When I was speaking at the NASW national conference in Washington, DC, I was asked, "What do you think of prolonged exposure?"

I answered succinctly, "I think it is prolonged." There was laughter. I often wondered, although it is accurate, why it was named *prolonged exposure*, because the only thing I would want to be prolonged is a massage.

While visiting an army base, I was invited to try out their prolonged exposure virtual reality equipment. Here you sit at a device and wear videoscope goggles. It also stimulates other senses; for example, when a bomb explodes in the scene, the chair vibrates. The person running the equipment for the soldiers who used it as part of their prolonged exposure treatment said, "They hate me." Those soldiers, in using this equipment, are exposed to more than what was in their actual memory of the event.

There are several programs that use ART with veterans including Warrior Wellness, The Lone Survivor Foundation, Warrior Mission: At Ease, and Warrior Rizen Ranch.

In these early days (2012) of attempting to bring knowledge about ART out into the general public, there were many clinicians who, once they were trained, became very excited about the therapy results. Some were skilled and professional, excited about how they transferred that knowledge, and others were more carried away by their enthusiasm. This particular group of high-ranking military medical servicemen and servicewomen had already been put off by the repercussions of an overly eager clinician pushing servicepeople to insist on getting ART in their military therapy sessions.

This unfortunate chain of events occurred during a time when there was a steady influx of "the next best thing" coming at them from all directions. One can easily understand how, being bombarded, the recipients of all of these suggestions became desensitized to new approaches. This attitude was strikingly apparent as the officials in the group looked at their watches more than they looked at me.

However, one of these officials, who attended after reading our first study, published in *Military Medicine* (Kip et al., 2013), was intrigued by what he read. It seemed to me, to the others' dismay, he wanted to be trained in ART. At the conclusion of that talk, this official that was most open and curious (and who I suspect initiated the first training) stated to his colleagues, "Who brings us a randomized controlled study? I'm interested. I'm intrigued, and I would like to train in this therapy." Later, he also said to me that he knew that somehow this kind of change in the brain could be done.

As a result of that military official's curiosity and interest in ART, a clinical training was arranged. The training room was filled with officials who lined up along the spectrum of deep interest to deep skepticism. However, as the three days of training ensued, a tangible shift toward surprise and even amazement took place. For example, after a live demonstration and a viewing of one of the videos of an ART session, one of the participants slammed his hand on the desk and stated, "Now I'm on board!"

Another military official followed us out into the parking garage at the conclusion of the training. He stated, "I've been a dedicated PTSD treatment expert for thirty years, and you waltz in here with this therapy!" He also shared that the military has spent millions of dollars on other attempts to treat PTSD that didn't prove to be effective.

Some military installations have us return repeatedly. At the conclusion of trainings at two bases, we were called to the front of the room, and the base commander awarded us Commander Coins of Excellence. We are very proud to be helping our military to ameliorate the epidemic of PTSD. We've done a multitude of ART trainings for the army and have begun working with other branches of the military.

In one experience, a supervisor urged one of the servicemembers to volunteer (they call it *volun-told*), and he agreed to be part of my live demonstration. Prior to my doing the demo, I went to the restroom. He followed me out into the hall and said adamantly, "I'm not going to fake this, you know."

"I wouldn't expect you to fake it," I replied.

During the demo he allowed himself to become emotional, obviously genuinely experiencing changes. At the completion of the session, he pointed his finger at the group and said, "You'd better listen to this woman very closely!" I then noticed that his whole demeanor had changed. He was smiling and laughing along with everyone else.

We have trained hundreds of seasoned military clinicians at many US military bases and locations including Walter Reed National Medical Center, Fort Belvoir Community Hospital, Fort Stewart, Fort Benning, Fort Bragg, Fort Hood, Naval Air Station Lemoore, Fort Drum, Fort Campbell, Tripler Army Medical Center, Eglin Air Force Base, and the Idaho National Guard.

## Chapter Fifteen

# ART BREAKING NEW GROUND IN OTHER MENTAL HEALTH SETTINGS

**THOUSANDS OF PSYCHIATRISTS AND** clinicians in private practice and various entities have been trained in ART.

We have traveled to train clinicians throughout the United States and Canada, including the University of Calgary. We've also trained at a university in Scotland. Additionally, many clinicians throughout the world have traveled to the US for ART training.

They have come from the United Kingdom, Italy, Australia, New Zealand, and Ireland. We've also trained clinicians at Betty Ford Clinic, The Refuge (FL), Western New England University, The Connection (CT), Crosswinds Counseling and Wellness

Center, Walden Behavioral Health, Connecticut Department of Mental Health and Addiction Services (DMHAS trained 42 clinicians.), Mission Health (NC), Previdence, Trinity Health/ Mercy Hospital (MA), and UConn.

We have recently trained mental health nurse practitioners from Yale New Haven Hospital. The Director of Nursing, LaRon Nelson, has been applying for grants to support a study that focuses on the efficacy of ART.

LaRon related a story about how he became interested in ART. He explained that one day he was waiting outside in the parking lot at University of South Florida College of Nursing. He noticed a woman, presumably a caregiver, trying desperately to coax a man out of the car and into the building. LaRon did not see that there was any observable danger in the parking lot; yet the man appeared beleaguered and terrified. The man eventually managed to get outside of the car, but then clutched onto the door and pressed his body against the car as if for safety. Whatever was the matter, the man could not easily bring himself to leave that vehicle, even though he wanted to and was trying to do so. Given that this was not an emergency, LaRon proceeded into the building to begin his workday.

Several days later he saw the same duo, but this time, the man and woman both exited the car without incident. This time the man did not require coaching, and he did not seem to be under any duress. In fact, he looked eager to leave the car and proceed to wherever he was going. LaRon compared this scene with the disturbing scene he had witnessed only a few days earlier. Something was up … and he wanted answers. He followed up to try and see what the reason was behind this person's change.

He eventually discovered that the man had been part of a study on Accelerated Resolution Therapy that was being conducted at the university. The man experienced dramatic immediate relief from his posttraumatic stress symptoms in response to the treatment. This is what led LaRon to become interested in ART and its applications to the treatment of traumatic psychological stress from a range of sources, including climate disaster-related trauma, stigma-induced trauma, and the psychological trauma of anti-Black structural violence. He has continued to apply for funding in order to further study ART so that its efficacy can be even more deeply established.

We trained forty-two clinicians for the state of Connecticut. Since we do a three-to-one training ratio, three trainees in a practicum group with one trained ART clinician, we had a very large training. The state Department of Mental Health and Addiction Services (DMHAS) funded the training with federal funds. We were delighted. They had more clinicians sign up for the training than we had room for, and we hope to have another training one day.

I was asked to do three follow-up consultations after the training, several months apart. We had almost full attendance for these, which I was told was unusual, and many spoke about their amazing results. They also had the opportunity to inquire how to use ART for different types of problems.

*Chapter Sixteen*

---

# PERSPECTIVE

**IN THINKING ABOUT LIFE'S** perspective, we can help a client look at their issues through new perspectives and think outside of the box. For example, I remember when I went into my older brother's bedroom to ask him a question. The question changed when I saw that he was sitting at a desk that had been stacked on top of another desk, his head almost touching the ceiling. I asked him, "What are you doing?"

He said, "I had a writer's block and needed a new perspective."

Another time I saw my brother's ingenuity in giving an object another perspective was when he was attending Princeton University. I walked into his house and saw the record player dangling from the ceiling from four strings. I asked him, "What is this?"

He replied, "I had to come up with a new way so that the record didn't skip when we walk across the floor." In those days, the needles would "skip" on the vinyl disk if there was too much vibration in the room. His solution may sound strange, but for me that seemed relatively normal. It made a lot of sense to me.

As an older teen I took a movie camera and shot close-up pictures of objects, asking, "What is this?" As I moved the camera back, the object came into focus, and it became clear what the object was. Some people could put the pieces together sooner than others. It was an interesting way to look at objects from a different perspective.

There were and are times when my creativity gets me into trouble. The first book report I ever did in first grade was about rocks. I cut paper into spirals and created a pop-up book. I received a C-. When I questioned the teacher about the low grade, she said, "Where are the facts?" "But the rocks pop up," I answered. My creativity was not enough; it would not always get me by.

When ART therapists, referring to my creative bent, tell me, "I'd love to be in your brain," I tell them, "That's fine, but you might not balance your checkbook!"

I have a framed Will Roger's saying, "Everyone is ignorant; only on different subjects."

With ART, as clinicians, we don't have to work as hard as in traditional therapy to help a client to change perspective. The eye movements change perspectives as the images are erased from view and replaced with positive images. The statement that a clinician likes to hear from a client is "I never thought about it that way before," or "I never looked at it that way before." It's all about opening up opportunities to have a different perspective.

Prior to developing ART, while using traditional talk therapy, I told some clients who tended to dwell on their "war stories" that we needed to limit the amount of repetition. For example, if a client kept telling me stories about a spouse's lying, the point would already have been clearly made early on, without all the repetition. What the client really needs to look at is the pattern. It is thinking about the pattern that can improve future behavior. When I'm with such clients, I might ask, "Where do you want to be in a year? Do you want to be in the same place, just having more war stories?" Then we would begin talking about what the client can do about the situation.

During ART sessions, later in my career, the war stories became scenes that could be quickly processed out. They had become a means to an end, no longer just spewing out the same thing over and over. Recounting the stories without using ART might make the client feel better for the moment, but it could take a long time and many repetitions to make the needed changes. For me, my dwelling on my childhood stories took years before I became desensitized. Now with ART, clients can feel that shift rapidly.

Often a client can review their perspective on their childhood abuse in one session. There is a video I have shown during trainings which does just that. The client realizes on her own, with the application of the eye movements, that she would not have been who she is today had it not been for that childhood. She now not only realizes but deeply feels that her strength emerged out of her past. She also begins to remember and focus on the positives from her childhood instead of the negatives. She relates to the negative few years with her stepfather as "grains of sand" in the big picture.

At the end of my private practice sessions I like to show an antique optical illusion to my clients. I have two little metal men. One looks bigger until you switch their positions and then the other looks bigger. They are actually the same size. I ask the client, "Which one looks taller?"

They say, "Fritz," but when I switch their positions around, then they say, "Paul." Even when they know they are the same size, the one positioned on the left always appears bigger.

I have another illusion in my home. I have displayed a face of a Buddha, and as you walk past the eyes, the whole entire face seems to turn and follow you. Even when you know what's behind the illusion, a part of the brain still becomes surprised.

I had a client who did the *Fear Flip* Script and saw a woman being sawed in half in her mind. I said, "But it's an illusion: her feet are really in the front of the box."

At the end of the session the client said to me, "I think I can face life's illusions now." She also said, "I don't think I've ever been broken. I've only made bad decisions." In other words, she just needed to make better decisions, which was "doable."

This reminds me of what people think about trust. When people say, "You either trust or you don't," that is difficult to work with, but when someone says, "There are things that I trust about a person and things that I don't trust," it is easier to resolve something about someone, as it is not "all or nothing."

There was a Vietnam veteran who would twitch every time he talked about going into the tunnels to set the charges on the bombs. He was always the first one in. When he did ART on this, he remembered something funny about it and started to laugh. ART often accentuates the positive in any scene, if there is any positive to be found. He remembered a videographer who was videotaping a charge he had just set, watching it burn. When he realized, the veteran went back to the hole and told the videographer, "What are you doing? Get your ass out of there!"

The man responded, "Huh?"

I pointed out that he had saved the cameraman's life. He barely made it out of the hole and was blown back. The client chuckled when he remembered the man's expression and exclaiming, "Huh?" Clients often comment "I never thought I would laugh about that!"

When we did the SUDS (Subjective Units of Distress Scale) at the end of the session, he only went down to a two. I asked what that was about. He said he thought he needed to keep some of the twitches in order to keep himself safe and honor the memory. However, I told him that with ART we focus on vigilance, not hypervigilance, which relies on thinking rather than reacting. I asked him to focus on the thought that we say "Keep the Knowledge, Lose the Pain." In this case, he lost the twitches. He came out with a slogan, changing "No pain, no gain" into "No pain, just brain." His twitches at that point were gone.

I had never thought of myself as a public speaker until I developed ART. It had become easy to speak about ART with my passion and also a perspective I developed as I thought to myself, *I am teaching magic tricks the brain can do.* I imagine the therapy wrapped up in a bow tie, and some comment on the neat packaging of the therapy combining its unique techniques with a gestalt approach, guided imagery, eye movements, and going back to the past as a psychodynamic therapist would do. And as a teacher I imagine I am doing "show and tell" to my therapist audience as I disclose a quick and what I consider easy approach to trauma and other mental health problems.

This mind-set has helped me overcome any fears about spreading ART. And I enjoy seeing therapists come to the realization that therapy can be done as a process without much content and takes the load off their shoulders.

I had a client who felt very guilty after his divorce because he felt that, by marrying his wife, he had subjected his children to an abusive person. In response to this, I first stated the obvious, "You would not have had these children that you love so much had you not been with that particular person," and I used a set of eye movements to have him reflect on that simple truth.

I then pointed out that he had told me repeatedly how well the children had turned out. "We are a product of all our experiences, and you tell me your children are wonderful, and you have no problems with them." I suggested that he take careful note of that, as he followed my hand to do another set of eye movements.

He then said, very excitedly, "I get it. I'm done. Thank you so much. I've struggled with this for the longest time, and that felt right. That is the answer, and I can move on now." I too have reached this kind of acceptance of my past, with an eagerness to move on.

*Chapter Seventeen*

# KEEP THE KNOWLEDGE, LOSE THE PAIN

**I HAVE HAD RELATIONSHIPS** in my life where others' lies and their distortions have played with my reality and the reality of others. For example, my first husband tampered with my reality by falsifying documents. He was a pathological liar.

With ART we change stories in our minds. But we know they are not "real" but more like using our imagination to create a dream, and we are not creating a false memory. It is crucial to know that we are not changing the facts about what really happened, while the images and affect do change.

While the client is creating their "good dream," using ART, they are still retaining all of the facts. They may even find more facts about the memory that were clouded by trauma before they engaged in ART. Because of this, early on, Amy and I came up with the phrase that captures this process: "Keep the Knowledge, Lose the Pain."

*Chapter Eighteen*

---

# BEYOND TRAUMA

## COVID, Phobias and more

*COVID Symptoms*

**THREE MONTHS AFTER TESTING** positive for COVID-19, a client presented with the long-haul symptom of losing her senses of taste and smell. She had come in to see me for a different problem which I took care of in a session. Then I asked if she would like to work on the symptom of lost senses due to COVID. She agreed, and I used ART's ability to make connections very quickly. I connected her ability to smell and taste to imagining memories of how she could taste and smell before she ever had COVID. We spent about fifteen minutes processing.

At the end of our session, the client reported that she had some sense of taste returning! I asked her to call me if she could taste her dinner. The next day she called and said that she had 80 percent of her taste and smell back. Excited, I told her she could come back to work on the other 20 percent (I never give up!). When she came back to see me the next day, I did a complete ART session on having COVID including erasing any negative images that she related to this. At the end of our session she agreed to taste an apple. She reported that she could taste the apple so thoroughly that she noticed that it was not a very good one. I gave her a mint, and she told me immediately she had full sensations of taste and smell of the wintergreen mint. She said wintergreen was her favorite flavor. She then exclaimed "I am in shock that this worked!"

*Loss of Sleep*

A client had reported to me that he had not had a good night sleep in thirty years. He was afraid of darkness approaching because of the nightmares he was having. There is a saying, "I took a bullet for you." In this case the client's best friend had stepped in front of him thirty years ago and actually taken a bullet for him and died.

This had haunted my client ever since. In doing ART he was able to process through the memory and erase the negative images. Then, using ART's Gestalt approach, he was able to say goodbye to his friend. His friend assured him (in his mind) that he was okay and that the client should also be all right.

Although this client was easily able to change his negative images, there are times when clients struggle to let go of a negative image. They may believe they are not being respectful to or honoring the person by letting go. I ask the question, "Who wants to be remembered by their worst possible moment?" During a set of eye movements, I ask the client to ask the person they lost how they would like to be remembered.

The client called me back to report that he had not had a nightmare in the three weeks since the ART session. He was planning to go back to work. He had given up smoking and had not had any urge to use a substance that he had previously struggled with.

He did want to return for another session in order to process out the anxiety from this quick change and his nervousness about returning back to work. He said others had noticed positive differences in him, and he was, as many clients say, shocked that one session had resulted in the change and in his ability to now sleep peacefully at night.

The guilt he had felt before was gone, and he was looking forward to resuming his life. He did not return for another session, yet he referred several relatives and let me video a follow up in which he describes how ART changed his life.

*Balloon Phobia*

When the client was about six years old, she went to a party with her dad, and all the other dads were popping balloons with their kids. The noise and surprise scared her. She developed a phobia about balloons. As an adult she cried, "I'm an adult and I can't deal with balloons!" I explained to her that it wasn't her, it was her "little-girl self," and we needed to "go back there" on a rescue mission.

We "went back there," and she took her little girl away from that problematic scene. After the session, we brought balloons into the room. I asked her if someone could pop a balloon, and she agreed. She had very little reaction. I emphasized that you can't control other people, just your own reaction. She connected this to some difficulty that she had with her dad's judgment. At the end of the session, I asked her how low her SUDS were, and she went to a 0.5. I asked her what that was about. She said it was to keep some control. I responded, "Zero means that you are in complete control, because you can completely control your reaction."

She was surprised by the change in perspective of the meaning of zero and said, "But you make sense, and now I have to go to zero!" She did a good job controlling her reaction of agreeing with me.

*The Elevator*

During a training, I did a live demo on someone who had an elevator phobia. We were staying in the same hotel. She was anxious to try going on the elevator once the session was finished, to see if it really worked. Murphy's Law cropped up; the hotel had lost power. She had to do what she has always done, take the stairs. The next morning, she did ride the elevator up and down several times quite happily. My suggestion to her was, while doing an eye-movement set, to envision in her mind hanging pictures of those she loved in the elevator and having a party in there. She was also invited to do anything she wanted. She chose the pictures and the party; the changed images "positized" her affect, and her phobia was gone.

When I had done ART with a twelve-year old who also had an elevator phobia, she turned it into the elevator ride at an amusement park. Following the session, her mother took her on an elevator. As they exited, she said to her mother, "We're supposed to try an elevator." There was a particular elevator that we had chosen.

But her mother pointed out, "You just rode on an elevator!" Now she looked forward to riding on elevators.

*A Client, Autism Spectrum, and ART*

While I was working for a psychiatrist, I had a client who was on the autism spectrum. He thought he should be in therapy, but he didn't really know why. I decided to ask him to "go to Oz" in his mind, using the eye movements, and ask the Wizard what he needed. After the eye movements, thinking concretely, he reported that he could not ask the wizard because "He was just a man behind a curtain!"

After the session, he was preparing to make another appointment. He called me over and said he didn't want me to think he was on LSD, but since the session he was seeing things in color. Apparently, prior to our session, he was only aware of seeing in black and white. I reassured him that it was fine. I thought it was a wonderful outcome, if the only thing this client gleaned from ART was that he was now recognizing color.

About a year later I reflected back on that session. I realized that the movie, *The Wizard of Oz*, is in black and white until Dorothy arrives in Munchkinland to begin her journey to Oz. This gave me the idea to use the Oz metaphor with another client. In a session with a woman who struggled with low self-esteem, from a mother who continuously put her down, she had some amazing results. By the end of the session, she said she felt authentic, even though she had always felt like she was being a phony in her life. I invited her to take herself to Oz and notice that, as she was in the black-and-white part of the movie, when she got to Oz (and became authentic) it would turn to color. When she went to see the Wizard, she reported afterward, she told him that she didn't need his advice because she knew where she was going now.

*Any Limbic System*

There was a dog who could not tolerate being approached from the front when someone was coming forward to pet him. So I wanted to have the owner move the dog's eyes back and forth with a dog treat in their hand while I approached the dog from the front. I believe that my approaching the dog brought up the fear memory while the owner's hand movements caused the dog to engage in the eye movements. After a few approaches, the dog calmed down and allowed being petted from the front. We know from science that eye movements have a calming effect on the brain. This proved to me that the eye movements have a calming effect on any being that has a limbic system, even a dog.

## Strokes

I have used ART with clients who addressed the psychological trauma around the stroke. Two could not walk heel to toe. By erasing the negative images of the stroke from view, and doing several other ART interventions, they were surprised, as was I, that they quite easily could walk the heel-to-toe strides. One of these was a clinician who was in an ART training just as an observer. She had a trauma therapy dog by her side. It did not leave her side, and she said it would not leave her. There was a time when she was home when the dog went to someone else because it felt her trauma. After I applied the ART protocol for about a half hour, her dog left her side as she easily took her walk, heel to toe. It appeared the dog was looking for her as it went by the chair she had been sitting in. It then spent time sniffing its way around the room. It had recognized her trauma was lessened or gone. It recognized a change.

Having the stroke victim erase the past trauma memories and practice, in their mind, the improvements they want to make, works well. I get excited and surprised each time.

In October 2020 I worked with a Vietnam veteran who had fifty years of reliving his trauma in his mind and dreams. He had talk therapy but was still symptomatic and had a stroke several months prior to my working with him.

We used the ART protocol to eliminate the negative images of Vietnam. I heard about one incident only from his daughter-in-law. In this incident, an object flew toward him. He saw it coming but had no chance to move. The current issues he was having also included an inability to move, and he would walk with fear, shuffling his feet. His wife would hold him up by his belt and walk with him. He also used a cane. He was frozen on the left side of his body.

After the session was complete, I asked the client if he wanted to try to walk. He said he was curious to try. Anytime a client is curious to confront a phobia or try something they were afraid to do, it has worked.

He stood up, and much to his amazement he was steady on his feet. His daughter-in-law said she had not seen him walk steadily on his feet for a very long time. He was also able to use his left arm. He wiggled his hand and fingers and stated he was "over the top" with joy that he had his mobility back. Enhanced trainees view a video of this event.

His wife came in, saw his improvements, and put her hand over her mouth in shock at seeing his walking and gaining his strength back in his arm. He walked up the stairs to take a nap after the session, something he could not do alone prior to the session. We have been told that he continues to improve and is now driving.

This work brings me so much joy in seeing the joy in others. Clients sometimes call it a miracle. I would love to see a study on using ART with stroke victims.

## Connecting Concepts

As I continued to evolve in my development of ART, I also realized that concepts and emotional states can be connected as easily as word meanings can. That is, I observed that the brain seems to be able to connect two concepts with the help of the eye movements and also can eliminate the connection between two concepts when they are not helpful.

I was surprised that many clinicians during my trainings had problems with dyslexia. We read a script, and they were having problems with the flow and understanding as they read. Video of this is also shown at Enhanced Trainings.

The first time I used eye movements to treat trauma associated with dyslexia was with a clinician who took two hours to read the one-hour script for the practicum. I took her on a break and using my intuition just asked her to "spread some peanut butter over the words." She said, "How did you know I love peanut butter and eat it every day?" I didn't know. It was just the first thing that came into my mind.

We did eye movements as she spread the smoothness of peanut butter over the words in her mind. I said a few more things that made sense to me. She returned to the practicum the next day and read the next script with no problem. Her intonation was the same as everyone else. Everyone was astounded, especially the trainee.

I have tried this a dozen more times. It always works, so I created a script for dyslexia. Other ART clinicians have reported that they have used it successfully. It seems to me that the people we have helped were stuck in the phonetic stage of learning how to read and that this "stuckness" caused trauma throughout the rest of their life. They painfully sound each word out and focus on the sound so by the time they have finished, they have lost the thread of what they are reading. Several years after I helped that trainee, I received a text thanking me again and telling me that she is still doing well.

A very excited ART therapist called after a training. They used the dyslexia script with a trainee whose first language is Spanish, and the trainee read better in both Spanish and English. The class was amazed.

Another time, I helped a trainee who was troubled by dyslexia his entire life and having trouble with the ART scripts. After about 20 minutes during a break, he read flawlessly to the group and cried because he could now read to his children.

I believe we are connecting emotional states together in the brain which can make a profound change in the way the brain functions. I have even helped a twelve-year-old stop reversing his letters. On the short follow-up with his teacher, I did find that he had written something with only one reversal. I would like to continue to work with this protocol for many different problems.

## Breaking Negative Connections

Negative connections can be undone using ART. For example, while helping at a retreat for veterans with PTSD, I worked with a veteran who had been a medic in the army. The veteran could no longer eat his wife's delicious (as he described it) spaghetti. His brain had made a connection between the image of the spaghetti and sauce to the image of parts of the bodies that he had worked on.

I asked him to "visit a spaghetti factory" and "see" how spaghetti was actually made (in his imagination with eye movements). He imagined seeing the flour, water, and egg transformed into spaghetti strands. He saw the sauce being made in big vats. Three weeks after the session, he sent me a text thanking me after he had just finished eating "a delicious bowl" of his wife's spaghetti.

*Another Example of Disconnecting a Negative Connection*

I did a live demonstration at a training with a woman who had a fear of birds. She had developed the phobia as a little girl after seeing Alfred Hitchcock's horror movie *The Birds*. We started our session with her agreeing to view a segment of that movie on a cell phone. She turned away from the phone and was in distress. Using the *Director*, I suggested she visit the movie set with Alfred Hitchcock, showing her that the "birds" were just actors. As her anxiety waned through the ART protocol, she started to see the birds on a wire, looking similar to the birds in Walt Disney's movie *Cinderella*. The birds were singing and happy. As these images changed, she became desensitized and then "positized." This allowed her cognition to change naturally from "birds are bad" to "birds are good."

At the end of the session, we showed her a clip from *The Birds*, and she was free of any negative sensations. She went home that night, and for the first time, she volunteered to feed their pet bird. When she moved her hand into the cage, the bird bit her! This would have been her worst fear before the ART session. Instead, she came in the next day and reported to the training group that when she tried to feed the bird, it bit her, "It must have been afraid of me. I will have to take my time and allow it to get used to me."

## The Frying Pan

Grandparents came from out of state with their teenaged grand-daughter, who had been having twenty psychogenic seizures per day for four years. They had heard about me.

I asked the teen, "What are you thinking about all day?" She replied that her father had been knocked out by her stepmother, who hit him with a frying pan. Her answer was quick and sure. I helped her erase those images, and she replaced them with better images of her choosing. The grandparents came back several weeks later to report that their granddaughter had not had one seizure since visiting with me. They were amazed. I was sure that getting rid of the problem images was the key. I was excited for her that she was going to have her life back.

## Addressing Pain and Uncomfortable Sensations

I was traveling home on a plane. There was a Spanish-speaking couple next to me. He stood up and held his heart. I said, "What's going on? Is he having a heart attack?"

"Oh, he is just having a panic attack, he hates to fly."

I knew I could try another protocol that I had developed, Sensation Awareness Focused Technique (SAF-T) and asked, "Would you like me to try to help?"

"Yes."

"Just ask him to follow my hand." And she did. He followed my hand. After the set of eye movements, looking puzzled, he sat down, opened the shade on the window, and pointed to the scene outside. Later when the plane began to land, he looked at me. I said, "Follow," and did two more sets of eye movements, and he relaxed again. I always wondered if they thought I was a witch—hopefully a good witch.

As the reader can see, in the story above I did not do an "ART" session. Just using the eye movements for calming works very well for first responders, nurses, employees in the ER, bachelor-level crisis mental health workers, coaches, massage clinicians, chiropractors, dentists, and any profession in which calming would be a benefit.

Non-licensed professionals and anyone who has someone in their life who needs to ameliorate uncomfortable sensations can be helped by SAF-T. I developed a special training for teaching SAF-T and invite all non-licensed helping professionals to learn how to use SAF-T in a one-day training. If any uncomfortable emotional material should arise, the helper is trained to calm the person and refer them to a licensed clinician, preferably an ART clinician, to work on the emerged issue.

During a SAF-T training that Amy conducted, a professional clinician volunteered to take part in the demonstration. He had been experiencing foot pain for years following an accident he was involved in. He did not share any details of the accident. She followed the manualized protocol for SAF-T, and he was amazed at the movement and transformation of the pain as it became metaphorically a part of a new story he created. At the conclusion of the demonstration, Amy advised him to consider seeing me for a full-blown ART session to make sure that he got to the root of what caused this metaphorical pain, including any psychological issues associated with the incident. This is an example of how we draw a boundary between SAF-T and ART. I saw him shortly after this, and he had a successful ART session.

Pain is a sensation. Sensations can be transformed. People take aspirin and other medications to block and alleviate pain so that the brain perceives the pain in a different way. I believe the reason why ART's eye movements also alleviate pain is by changing pathways in the brain, possibly the way medications do. Dr. Kevin Kip was surprised that there was a change in pain levels in his ART studies. He did a study on the direct experience of pain for those in a support group who had tried everything and were still experiencing significant pain. After engaging in ART, their pain as a whole decreased, and that is encouraging (Kip et. al., 2016). Hopefully, in the future there will be more studies on ART and pain.

I did ART with a client with a soccer injury who was afraid to get rid of his pain for fear he would not realize when he was further injuring himself. He eventually wanted to try it for the pain. What he found was that the sharp pain was not there. He did notice a sensation that communicated to him what he needed to know about his body, but he would not describe it as pain.

Another client came back for a second session because he could still see himself "rolling through the windshield" from his car accident. He still had pain. Once we erased the image of him rolling through the windshield, much to his surprise his pain decreased significantly. I think these negative images are metaphorically telling us there are still images to be erased and stories in the brain that can be reevaluated and "retold" to aid with the metaphorical pain.

I had a nun as a client. She slowly walked into my office with the support of a walker. She explained she had been falling frequently and had great difficulty in walking. During the session her legs became heavy. I invited her to imagine that she put balloons under her legs, and they did feel lighter. When the session, which involved childhood abuse, was completed, she walked to my door. "I don't think I need this walker," she commented, and she gave the walker to her companion. In a follow-up, she told me that she had been walking briskly and moving up and down stairs with ease. She agreed to be on a television news spot with me.

Apparently, her inability to get around had been getting worse and worse until she needed a walker. It was the metaphorical way in which her brain was telling her she had something from her past to process. I believe many of our physical ailments and mental health issues are metaphorical, and they are our bodies way of alerting us to those problems from the past that need to have resolution.

*Chapter Nineteen*

---

# OTHER INTERVENTIONS

## Going Fishing: Trichotillomania and Skin Picking

**I HAVE DEALT WITH** trichotillomania (anxiety expressed through pulling out one's hair) two times with two different clients. One of the clients not only pulled her hair but also picked at her skin.

For each client I used a metaphor that appeared to be helpful for the clients. With the eye movements, I had them drop a fishing line into the water in their mind and pull up whatever they could. Both clients said that "nothing" came up. I said "Exactly." This translated to "Why do this, because it isn't helpful?"

I asked the client who did both hair pulling and skin picking to "pull" another activity out to "wallpaper" over the image of her pulling of her hair. I used eye movements because using a word with two different meanings, while doing the eye movements, helps call the subconscious forward while the conscious mind is busy trying to figure it all out. It also changes a negative meaning to a positive meaning. With this client who did both, I asked her to "pick" another activity and yet still later to "pull" another activity as a way of engaging more of that wordplay.

## Major Disaster Trauma

A first responder who was on the scene both at 9/11 and the Sandy Hook Elementary School shooting came to see me to treat his trauma. We resolved 9/11 in the first session. When he came in for the second session in order to address his trauma from the Sandy Hook incident, once we had started the eye movements for this session, he said that he noticed that the first session had taken care of this trauma as well (the benefits had generalized).

## Fear Flip Intervention Wordplay

I long realized that I needed a script for clients who were afraid of change. I was in Canada doing a training, and someone suggested, "What about a changing room?" I had remembered an intervention I had developed called *The Room*. During this Advanced ART training, which can be less structured than the Basic training, a clinician expressed her displeasure that it was less structured. I feel that the Advanced training has a structure to it. She didn't agree.

I asked her if she feels uncomfortable when her day is unstructured, and she agreed that was true. I said that sometimes after going through a school system where you are structured and then in a work environment that is structured, people may have a problem going from structured to "unstructured." I asked her if I could try something with her as a demonstration and created a new script on the spot that I call the *Fear Flip*.

The idea to call this intervention the *Fear Flip* came from the show Flea Market Flip. On this show two teams of contestants go to a flea market and pick up items that can be updated and changed into repurposed, interesting, and often beautiful pieces. They then attempt to sell their "new" items at another flea market. Whichever team makes the most money wins the contest.

I thought of the *Fear Flip* as flipping a fear of change into an anticipation of a brighter future, using the wordplay between *fear* and *fair*. With the eye movements, the clients imagine picking up change at the beginning and end of the journey. They turn their anxiety into excitement about the future and feel better able to handle the challenges once they leave their fair (fear) behind.

When doing the *Fear Flip* with the client, in the *fair* (fear) there are *past tents* (past tense—more wordplay), *present tents*, and *future tents*. The client can meet their future self and go to tents where they can make changes. At the end of my demonstration with her, she invited me to carry on with the training, and it did not seem to bother her that it appeared less structured to her. As a matter of fact, she commented, "Who cares about structure?"

I recently spoke with an ART therapist who deals with many who are suicidal. He uses the *Fear Flip* to help his clients meet their future selves. He is excited that this intervention helps them see a future.

## Lucid Dreaming

As mentioned previously, I believe ART can be similar to "lucid dreaming." A trained ART therapist, consulted with me about a case. It sounded as if the client was not ready to go back to her early traumatic childhood memories. I made some suggestions to lessen the anxiety and have the session done metaphorically, which I think is akin to "lucid dreaming." This was her follow-up:

> The ART therapist's client was very open to trying a different approach using the explorer metaphor. She envisioned taking a particular friend with her.
>
> We discussed her exploring uncharted territory for her future self as the captain of her ship. She explained that she has a significant fear of water and asked for a life jacket …. I felt that water/ sailing imagery would impede progress due to her fear of water so we used another analogy that was somewhat similar. She chose her favorite kind of car to drive but she seemed unable to explore anywhere new. She drove the car to faraway places but the roads were all familiar to her (to provide a sense of comfort and safety, she had her friend with her in the car and had a trinket in her pocket

that belonged to her a long time ago; she visualized her sister giving it to her as a symbol of luck and good fortune). Even with the item of comfort and her friend accompanying her, she experienced painful muscle cramping during the exploration up to this point so we changed things up a bit again ....

She said at this point that she was too scared to explore without a structured plan for where she would go ... she felt too vulnerable to carry on. At this point, I suggested that she could ride in a bulletproof/ shatterproof/ indestructible crystal-clear bubble that hovered. Only she had the controls for the bubble and access by anyone else was impossible because the bubble was designed only for her and whomever she chose to have with her. At all times, she alone was in control of where the bubble could go and nothing harmful could reach her there. She was able to steer the bubble anywhere she wanted so she could safely seek out the future while being protected at the same time.

For two sets of EMs (eye movements), she rode in the bubble (she still had some progressive muscle tightening but it was much less than earlier in the session) and was able to look around. The muscle spasms seemed to be causing physical pain so I suggested that we process those sensations (now that she had the safety of the bubble).

This time, from the safety of the bubble, she was able to process the sensations. After the EMs, she said that she felt the pain being pulled away or thrown off of her upper body. We decided to keep going. Her description of how the tension and physical pain were leaving her body sounded to me like a powerful magnet pulling the pain off of her. Continuing EMs, she described her pain in her lower body moving from 99 percent to 32 percent. She liked the magnet analogy and asked to keep going. The "magnet" was able to completely pull *all* of her physical pain away. She wept a lot at this point and said she had never felt free of the weight ever before. She also said she was afraid that the pain/severe muscle tightness would return.

I suggested more EMs where she would tell her muscles that they have carried all of the heaviness and pain for her all her life and have done their job in keeping her safe; now it is time for them to rest. Their job is over. She was able to do this successfully and experienced feeling calm.

Because she was so fearful of letting go of the anxiety, fear, and pain (because she perpetually felt there would be nothing left to her if she let go) ... I suggested another set of EMs where she visualized a tiny speck of light at the center of her heart ... and as she moved her eyes, she could visualize the lightness growing inside her until it reached every cell in her body and in her spirit. I told her that this perennial light that always existed in her was now able to grow in her and shine ... that it was taking over and replacing the pain that used to exist.

She said the light had reached every part of her and was radiating out of her. She cried heavily then and said she was "finally free"; she said she no longer feels like an object. She feels "human" for the first time ....

[T]hanks for chatting with me on Wednesday and for helping me help this woman when she was feeling so very stuck in her pain. I sincerely appreciate your help with this. Next week, we are going to attempt an ART session to process some of the early sexual abuse.

## Annoyance List Script

After a successful ART session on a trauma scene, a client showed me a list of problems he wanted to work on. I thought about it. Since ART is a procedure and does not get into content, I wondered if we could process the list as the problem. The fact that he had a list was the problem.

I had him read his list aloud. I processed the sensations that came up as he read the list. I added a few steps from the script I use for trauma with dyslexia. It worked, and at the end of the session he was able to rip up his list. He learned a lesson about how to handle future issues as a result of interventions in the script. He thanked me and said he was done.

When working with individual clients, after a successful ART session, I sometimes end with a client by doing the *Annoyance List*.

When I do my final day of Enhancement training with ART clinicians, and they are about to practice the *Annoyance List*, I make sure to tell them to add me to the list if I've done anything to annoy them during the training!

## Couples Treatment

I often see the couple initially for a thorough intake to see what the issues are. Most often a clinician hears, "It's a communication problem." We must boil it down from there to describe for the three of us what exactly that means. I usually then separate the couple and see each individually. I visualize a couple coming in with two individual "issue bags" and a third "bag" containing the couple's issues.

The *Annoyance List* is really a great intervention for couples treatment. Many couples come in due to annoyances with each other. If there are underlying issues, those can be addressed once the annoyances are dealt with. If the annoyance list is really the problem, then they can move forward with a renewed acceptance of one another.

## Retrieving Memories

I believe everything we have heard or seen may be stored somewhere in our brain. Unless there is an organic change, where parts of the brain are removed in some way or irreparably damaged, then the material may just be blocked from view. Since ART is so good at making new connections, I have had clients retrieve blocked information with the aid of the eye movements.

A client who had a stroke had memory issues. He and his wife said that he was especially bothered by not remembering names.

Having his wife read lists of five things to him and with the aid of some eye movements I asked him to repeat lists of fruit, and other groupings of things that had a connection to each other.

The client was able to retrieve two or sometimes three items when asked immediately to retrieve and recite what his wife had just said. The final list was comprised of five names. He retrieved only two.

I chatted with the client and his wife after the session for 15 min or so. I answered his wife's questions about ART and suddenly the client broke into the conversation and yells out the five names he had earlier been asked to retrieve, much to his, his wife's and my amazement.

I often see how the eye movements are helpful for retrieval. The ART procedures can erase traumatic images from view but also aid in retrieval. I believe future ART scripts can aid clients to learn and retrieve in a more expedient way.

When I lose my keys and move my eyes, I often see an image of where I last left them. I told my sons that when they have a test, if they forget an answer, they should look down, close their eyes and move them to see if they can retrieve that answer. Since ART is connected to a calming sensation in the brain, that also helps with test anxiety.

I did see a client who reported she had lost all her memories and could not even remember recent events or conversations. She had seen me once before for a different problem and hoped I could help her. The physicians said there was nothing cognitively wrong with her. The blocking of memories, they thought (and I agree), may have been a result of a coping strategy when she was younger that she developed for some reason she did not know. That coping strategy lingered around even after it was no longer needed. She now wanted her memories back. I used my clinical ART intuition and did a session with her, in a different way than I had done before. I took her to Oz to ask the Wizard for a key to her memories. After she got the key to unlock her memories, I suggested that she could sit down and view her past memories on a screen. The results are here in her words.

> I came into the session tonight hoping to retrieve past memories and to enhance my memory going forward.

> At the time of the session, I basically had no memories of my childhood, no memories of my son growing up (he's twenty-four now), and no memories of events or conversations that I've had as

an adult. One example that I mentioned at the beginning of the session was that I ran across a notebook one day that had a business plan written in it. I looked at the dates, and it had been written six months earlier. I had no recollection of writing it even though it was written in my handwriting. These types of things happened all the time and it was very frustrating.

By the end of the session, I was able to remember things from my childhood as well as events from my son's childhood. I was even able to remember a conversation I had with my son right before my session and a conversation I had with a girlfriend a week prior. I would have never been able to remember the specifics of these conversations before the work that was done in the session.

As I left the office and drove home, everything seemed crystal clear, as if I was seeing things for the first time. Whatever was keeping me from seeing and remembering had been completely cleared.

I am amazed that we accomplished all of this in one session. Prior to this, it was like I was living in the movie 50 First Dates. Every day was new, and I never brought any experiences with me from the previous days. Now, I am excited to have my life back and to be able to build upon the experiences that I have.

*Chapter Twenty*

# MORE ON SPIRITUALITY

**I MET MY LEAD** trainer, Amy Shuman, in 2009 in one of the first groups that I trained. I found it interesting that she told me that somebody with whom she had not been in contact for several years suddenly started emailing her persistently to take this ART training.

As a result, both my lead trainer and I were prodded—Amy by her colleague and me by my brother—in the direction to spread ART. We became best friends which we are to this day and traveled extensively to spread ART. One of her assigned duties as my best friend is to make sure I stay humble.

I really feel that ART is given to me from the Higher Power. As mentioned earlier, I don't practice within an organized religion, but I do have a spiritual base after having been in Al-Anon over those many years. I did ask Amy to say two words to me if she thought I was acting in a narcissistic way. And those two words are "sweat lodge." This is because at that time, a newly famed healer was alleged to have pressured his participants to stay in the sweat lodge too long, ignoring their protests, and this resulted in several tragic deaths.

I feel that I brag about ART like it's one of my children. I tell people I have three children, Zach, Josh and ART, and as the parent I feel I have bragging rights. People have tried to insist that I take the credit for ART development, but I don't want to hedge my bets. I am grateful to the Higher Power.

I was not sure I wanted to add anything about being spiritual into my book and the things that happened to me that could be called by some a "coincidence" or by some "spiritual." I do not practice my Jewish religion, but I do enjoy some of the customs. Being spiritual is different, I feel, because for me it means that the situations I find myself in and the things that happen to me are not necessarily coincidental but orchestrated by something greater than me.

Prior to becoming a clinician, I was in the Al-Anon program, a program for people who deal with or have dealt with someone's abuse or addiction to alcohol. I did not know what it was to be spiritual at that time. However, a central premise of Al-Anon is the recognition of a Higher Power. Some may say that the Higher Power has no time to show me that it exists. I was skeptical and was probably an agnostic for much of my early life.

The first thing I called a spiritual happening (and not a coincidence) was when my firstborn was just two years old. I had this thought that to be a good mother, one should bronze the child's baby shoes. I could only find one shoe. My husband and I were in a small apartment at the time, and I looked everywhere for the other shoe. I became obsessed with finding it and had that magical thinking that I couldn't be a good mother unless I found and bronzed them both. I gave a test to the Higher Power. "If there is a Higher Power then help me to find the baby shoe!" You may think this is crazy, but no one said people who develop new things are not a bit eccentric or even a bit "OCD."

A few days later I was leaving the apartment, and I went out the back door. I happened to look over to my right, and there were about a dozen plastic white garbage bags all tied up sticking out of the garbage cans. Poking out of the center bag was the tip of my son's shoe. I was so shocked that I never did bronze the shoes, as it didn't seem necessary once that had happened.

Another spiritual happening occurred when I finally moved back to my hometown. When I was twenty-one, and my mother passed, my younger brother and I had to leave our home when my father sold our house.

Since leaving my family home, I had always felt I wanted to move back to my hometown and was able to do that in my forties. After the purchase of my new home, the estate salespeople were about to finish clearing the house before we moved in. I asked them if I could pay them to leave what was still there behind because I might want some of it. After the closing, which was very meaningful to me, I literally kissed the ground before entering. I felt like I was truly "home" again, and I walked into the house for the first time as the new owner.

Perhaps the Higher Power guided me directly through the kitchen to the dining room. I knew that out of all the things left behind, I had to go to one particular dish that was shaped like a cauliflower. I had no idea why it was the very first thing I was drawn to. I was compelled to turn it over. On the bottom of this dish was written "hand made by Weil."

My mother's maiden name was Weil, and my cousins and I called ourselves "the squeaky Weils." I am the baby and the youngest squeaky Weil. To this day, I feel that the writing on the back of that dish meant my mother endorsed my house purchase and was happy I was there. I had looked for houses for over a year, and when I found this one, I knew it was right. Although it needed work and we had a loan amount that just qualified for the purchase, I knew it was home. It had elements that reminded me of our old family house. This was such a comfort to me as I had been quickly removed from my old home after my mother's death.

Another spiritual experience was that in my youth I met Judy, my older and wiser cousin, and right away I wanted to be closer to her. She guided me. She is the one who told me to go to Al-Anon. She helped everyone, even staying in touch with her ex's children as if they were her own. She lived in Florida where she had raised her four young sons on welfare and working hard, taking real estate classes, and ultimately with her husband owning the largest privately held real estate school in Central Florida.

As previously mentioned, Judy had great business sense and acumen. She created my training entity, the Rosenzweig Center for Rapid Recovery and ran it until her recent passing. I am so grateful I got my wish to be close to this amazing person.

During my teens and into my twenties I had learned Transcendental Meditation. I would meditate for fifteen to twenty minutes each morning and each evening. I had some experience with what seemed like clairvoyance. It scared me, and I hesitated to tell people about it. Sometimes I would test it out of curiosity.

My older brother visited from England. I said, "Why don't you stay in the kitchen? I'll go to a room at the end of the hall, and you think of an animal. I will try to see if I can guess what it is." As I stood in the bedroom I listened for the sound of an animal, freeing my brain up as much as I could from conscious thought. I heard "arrngatang" (orangutan) in my mind. Why I heard that instead of "monkey" is puzzling, but I clearly heard "arrngatang."

He exclaimed in a surprised tone, "I first thought of an orangutan, but then I changed it because I thought that would be too difficult." And then I guessed "hyena" which was his second choice. He confirmed both guesses with amazement.

Once I put some friends in a circle and asked the one next to me to write a three-digit number and pass it around. I asked everyone to think about it, and I was able to "guess" it correctly.

One morning while meditating, in my mind I saw my first husband walking with a coworker, and in my mind's eye I could see her fall. I called her and asked, "How are you?"

She replied, "Oh, your husband told you about the fall?"

I would feel remiss if I did not mention my spiritual story of the loss of my spouse of thirty-three years. He was swimming in a pool and died suddenly. I was in the attic prior to a work trip to retrieve something, and I leaned on the frame of a mirror, and it broke. I thought, *Oh boy! Who knows what will happen next!*

And I was right. What happened next was that I was helping the Lone Survivor Veterans with ART in Texas on the day of my husband's death. He had gotten up early that morning to drive me to the airport. Once I arrived, I wanted to call him to tell him that I arrived safely, and because there was no cell signal, I hiked up a hill and called him. He picked up, which was somewhat unusual for him to do during the workday. I asked him how he was feeling after having to wake up so early. He said, "I feel Grrr-eat!" I thought he sounded like Tony the Tiger. I ended that call reminding him to pick me up from the airport on Monday.

That night while the staff and I sat around a campfire, everyone but me saw a shooting star. I went inside and asked if I could use someone's computer to try and check in with my family. I noticed an email from my younger son. I opened it and read, "We have an emergency!"

I had a pit in my stomach, and I recalled that days earlier I had said to my husband, "You need to go the dentist because that toothache has been bothering you for a while. If you don't take care of it, it could go to your heart."

He said, "It's not an emergency," using that same word my son had used in his email. Alex did make an appointment, unfortunately it was on the day of his funeral.

I called my younger son's cell phone from the ranch's landline. He picked up and said, "Dad was swimming, and he didn't make it."

I said, "That makes no sense, I will call your older brother," because I didn't know what he was talking about. My older son confirmed that while swimming, Alex had passed away.

I shook and could not sleep the night I learned of his death. During the flight home, while sitting at the airport I received a phone call asking if I wanted to donate his eyes which I found surrealistic because in my mind he was still alive. I had to catch a tram because the plane connection was too tight, and I cried during the tram ride. I even told the woman next to me on the plane, "My husband's dead and I'm going to cry. I'm sorry."

She said simply, "Cry on," in a comforting and understanding tone.

Later, I needed to do some legal tasks related to his death. I wanted to find an attorney. I looked at a list of attorneys' names and chose one. It was strange that I chose him because he was an hour away; normally I would choose someone closer, but his name stood out. I called the number, and he picked up immediately. I told him about my husband's death, and he told me that he was an attorney who specialized in drownings. That was curious enough but then he asked, "Is it alright if I come and visit you tonight at your home?" I thought, *I don't even know this attorney, and he wants to come visit.* He said he had something to tell me.

I gathered my two sons together as we sat in the living room that evening across from this attorney. He told us, "I want to tell you that my law partner was there and saw your husband go under the water." He had been admiring how he had, as an older person, been diligently doing his laps. I was shocked. I had picked an attorney whose partner was in the pool on a Friday night with only a few others while my husband was swimming—an attorney who worked an hour away. *What are the chances?* I thought.

My husband's aortic aneurism, I learned, was such a big event that he could not have survived.

The funeral was difficult. I was numb, a normal sensation as my brain was protecting me from reality. People called me brave during the talk that I gave about Alex, but it was really the numbness and the disbelief that carried me through. Relatives came from England, Florida, and North Carolina, and I found that comforting, although it was a temporary way to ease the pain.

Of course, I always knew I could someday use ART and the eye movements to ease my sensations. Taking walks and moving my eyes was helpful. Having a dream where I could tell him I loved him was helpful.

At the funeral, my older son, Zach, gave a touching eulogy. My younger son, Josh, played his guitar and sang Leonard Cohen's song "Hallelujah." Coincidentally Josh had recently taken up guitar and had learned that song. I had told Alex shortly before I left for the ranch that "Hallelujah" was my favorite song. Josh, at college, was on the phone, and I asked him to play it on his guitar. Alex said, "Why are you playing that song?" He did not realize it was Josh playing. I told him, "He just learned it on the guitar!"

After the funeral, I was at my kitchen table, and from a place of pain, I spoke my husband's name three times out loud. The light bulb above the table made a bursting sound and blew out.

It seemed significant that he passed away on Pearl Harbor Day, December 7th, as a year earlier while visiting Josh in Hawaii, we visited Pearl Harbor and the Arizona monument. Alex was transfixed by the list of servicemen lost that day.

When I learned about his death, the person who spent the night with me before I traveled home, told me that when I sat at the table in the room below, the chandelier above was swaying back and forth with no wind. It spooked her, but she did not tell me about it until five years had passed. What it means, I'm not sure, but these are the facts.

The eye movements have helped me to cope and to process my tears. I choose to remember the positive, although I have the facts as all ART clients do; we know that the suffering can be eased. Instead of hearing the sad Leonard Cohen song, I now hear a song that is a more "joyful" sounding song to me, that my son also learned, called "Yellow" by Coldplay (2000). While the lyrics do get a bit dark further into the song, the beginning is what I remember:

> I wrote a song for you
> And all the things you do
> And it was called "Yellow"

I connect that joyful feeling to my memory of my late husband.

Another mirror broke followed by another death. I drove into my garage, and I heard a "crack." Was this another foreshadowing? I pulled back out of the garage and saw that my right-side rearview mirror had broken. I thought, once again, *Oh boy, I hope nothing bad happens.* My significant other, David, and I could not figure out why the glass broke, but the housing did not fall off. The next day I got a call from the police department telling me that my younger brother, who lived in North Carolina, had died.

On a happier note, years later David and I bought each other a Valentine's card. We bought the same one. He went to a different store, and out of all the possibilities, we exchanged the same card. I bought mine because I didn't want it to be too "over the top," just "cute." He handed me his card, saying he didn't want it to be too "shmaltzy." Same reason, same card. His first name (David) was my husband's middle name. His last name (Gordon) was my older son's middle name. At this writing we have been together for over seven years, and out of all the men I have dated, he is the right one. We visited a cemetery out of state where his parents and other family members are buried, and I thought it looked familiar. One of my cousins is buried a few feet away. Coincidence?

While traveling with my lead trainer, I talked about the fact that after my mother died, finding pennies on the ground became a significant sign of her presence to me. After this discussion, as we walked into the restaurant, right in front of the door was a penny.

While working with a particular client, in order to widen the breadth of their choices through ART, I said, "One of the things you can do is pull yourself out of the situation with a helicopter."

"How did you know my husband flew helicopters?" she said. I didn't, but I could see it in my mind.

One of the first videos that we show at a clinical ART basic training is that of a postal worker who could not deliver the mail after being mauled by a dog. I ask her at the end of the video, when she imaginatively goes over a bridge to leave her problem behind, "I bet there were walkways on the other side of the bridge." I could see them in my mind. She responded, "Yes, there are walkways, and it reminds me of Munchkinland" (in *The Wizard of Oz*).

Years later, she is still delivering mail as I encounter her from time to time at the post office.

During a training, a clinician was experiencing ART during the practicum. In his scene his father was hovering over him telling him he was a loser while he was wrestling. When he changed his scene, he reported he could see his Higher Power hovering over him instead of his father, and the Higher Power was encouraging him and comforting him. He told the group how he had just re-done his scene and how powerful it felt to experience his Higher

Power in that way. I said, "Yes, your Higher Power is with you!" as a loud clap of thunder shook the room.

This was followed by a complete silence for about ten seconds. He then said very slowly, "I will never forget this moment." Next, laughter filled the room as we all released the tension of that moment with its exquisite timing.

My intuition or clairvoyance—whatever someone wants to call it—seems to guide me when I am with a client. While practicing ART, many clinicians have reported that they get more in tune with their clients and develop this intuition. With or without intuition, the protocol just works. Either way, it's the client, not us, who determines what they need.

My spirituality is an important part of my life, so I've included it in this book. Some people ponder why, if there is a Higher Power, bad things happen. I don't have an answer for that question, although I am sure the universe has one. And when I face challenges, I sometimes wonder how they will turn out and wonder in the moment about this Higher Power and what Its motivation is. As do most people, at times I have felt what appears to be unbearable pain.

It is the spiritual intuition that guides me with clients and has contributed to the making of Accelerated Resolution Therapy. There are still questions, but I often feel what helps me is greater than me and is guiding me. It's just what I feel. Understanding my story may help you to understand how I developed ART, and so I include it in the book.

On April 3, 2021, I had a stroke while in Charlotte, NC attending to the estate of my younger brother, Mark. Although I would not wish a stroke on anyone, I had the best circumstances possible. David was with me and got me to the hospital immediately. He stayed with me during my hospitalization and has moved in to be my caregiver. He now helps with my business. Fortunately, my cognition was not affected, only my right arm, right hand, and right leg. I still see clients and helping them heal gives me great joy. I am able to put the positives over the negatives, and I am grateful every day for what I have.

*Chapter Twenty-One*

---

# EPILOGUE

**WHEN I THINK ABOUT** my choice to become a clinician, I ponder whether I have fulfilled a childhood need to be heard. My clients listen and respect my opinions. I have worked on my codependency issues over the years, and I hope that this need no longer plays a significant role in my life.

The fact that ART can so quickly turn negative to positive, get rid of negative images in one session, and bring wide smiles to clients who were in such pain, causes emotions in me that are difficult to describe. I know what it is like to feel depressed, and I know what it is like to feel normal, but it took me not one session but rather years to recover before I discovered ART. I have had panic attacks in my life and learned how to cope with them, but that took me years as well. I had an eating disorder and an addiction that were hard to recover from. I have experienced inappropriate sexual behavior, and that took me years to get beyond. I have been there and done all that, and now to have found the way to bring lightning-quick relief to so many, from these same kinds of problems, has been a wholly unexpected and an incredibly rewarding blessing.

If you want more information about ART and ART training, our websites are www.acceleratedresolutiontherapy.com or www.artworksnow.com.

My web site is www.erasetraumanow.com. Feel free to contact me via my email at yenal3523@yahoo.com.

Laney

## Researcher's Note

In 2010, as an associate professor at the University of South Florida (USF), I was extremely fortunate to have received a Congressionally-appropriated grant from the Department of Defense (DoD) in the amount of $2.1 million. The primary purpose of this funding was to study health effects and evaluate "alternative" treatment approaches for US service members, veterans, and their family members suffering from emotional distress from military service (e.g., US-led combat deployments in Iraq and Afghanistan).

As an epidemiologist with research training primarily in cardiovascular disease, I was not even quite sure how to spell psychotherapy. So, rather naively, I began searching for "alternative" treatment approaches that might extend beyond traditional "talk therapy," as well as those considered "first-line" and endorsed in formal Veterans Administration (VA) and DoD clinical practice guidelines. It is here where I stumbled upon Laney Rosenzweig and her very early use of Accelerated Resolution Therapy (ART), as described in a newspaper article that was sent to me.

So I invited Laney down to USF in Tampa to provide a one-hour seminar on ART and invited colleagues from across USF to attend, as well as health professionals in the areas of treatment of posttraumatic stress disorder (PTSD) and traumatic brain injury (TBI) from the nationally-recognized James A. Haley VA Hospital. While Laney's seminar was delivered with clarity and good presentation, at the end of the hour, comments and reactions from the attendees were generally muted, skeptical, or borderline hostile, yet curious and positive in some instances. From this initial meeting, I recognized immediately that ART would likely be perceived, at large, as not evidence-based and possibly as snake oil, despite the fact that the core elements of ART are consistent with core elements of established trauma-focused treatments for PTSD (Hoge and Lies, 2015).

Not to be disillusioned, as part of the Congressionally-appropriated grant funding, what motivated me to study ART as one of five funded projects was, in large part, a simple gut reaction to Laney as a mental health clinician. As a scientist, this was out of character for me. But I sensed a very high level of creativity and intuition in Laney, along with what I perceived as an innate gift in being able to identify and treat exact sources of distress in previously unknown individuals, no matter what the originating source. While Laney may not prefer this description, I sometimes describe her as somewhere between normal and eccentric; that is, overall, good functioning, yet somewhat of a savant in terms of the capacity to treat mental illness and related comorbidities.

So my journey to start conducting research on ART began in 2010 and in the ten years since has resulted in the completion of five research studies (as principal investigator or collaborator). While only two of these studies have been modest-sized randomized controlled trials, the gold standard design in clinical research, results from these studies have provided strong peer-reviewed scientific evidence that ART, evaluated within a research environment, results in substantial clinically meaningful reductions in symptoms of PTSD and related conditions or comorbidities in the majority of cases treated. In these research studies, the average length of treatment has been three to four sessions, which is much briefer than current "first-line" psychotherapies for treatment of PTSD.

The training of mental health clinicians in ART, now beyond five thousand practitioners worldwide, has clearly outpaced the modest amount of empirical research data published to date. Science in terms of acquisition of new knowledge can be notoriously slow, and sometimes when something is really good, such as an effective treatment modality, market forces tend to overshadow whatever science base exists. This is what I believe has happened and is continuing to happen with ART.

Of course, I simply hope that this book, and its firsthand account of Laney's journey in developing and disseminating ART, will continue to flourish in terms of applications of ART. As a scientist, I know that there is no substitute for rigorously conducted and documented research findings. However, I also know that having an open mind is essential to scientific discovery. When I teach epidemiological methods, one of my favorite quotes is from Sir Peter Medawar, a British biologist sometimes referred to as the "father of transplantation" (e.g., with respect to organ transplant rejection). He stated, "I cannot give any scientist of any age better advice than this: the intensity of the conviction that a hypothesis is true has no bearing on whether it is true or not" (http://nobelprize.org/nobel_prizes/medicine/laureates/1960/medawar-bio.html).

I interpret Sir Medewar's statement as, simply, "Always keep an open mind." As a researcher for twenty years, I know that science is often unpredictable. I believe that ART has great promise beyond its initial indication for treatment of PTSD, yet only time (and research) will tell its ultimate value and dissemination to so-called "off-label" indications.

I hope you have read this book with an open mind, bearing in mind its express purpose—that is, to contribute significantly to humanity at large.

Respectfully,
Kevin E. Kip, Ph.D.
April 29, 2020

Kevin E. Kip, Ph.D., FAAAS, FAHA
Distinguished USF Health Professor
College of Public Health, Population Health Sciences
University of South Florida
13201 Bruce B. Downs Blvd., CPH, Room 2108
Tampa, FL 33612

# References

Alberini, C. M., and J. E. LeDoux. 2013. "Memory reconsolidation." *Current Biology* 23 (17): R746–R750.

Brownell, P. 2010. *Gestalt therapy: A guide to contemporary practice*. Springer Publishing Company.

Buck, H. G., P. Cairns, N. E. BPharm, D. F. Hernandez, T. M. Mason, J. Bell, … and C. Tofthagen. 2020. "Accelerated Resolution Therapy: Randomized Controlled Trial of a Complicated Grief Intervention." *American Journal of Hospice and Palliative Medicine* 1049909119900641.

Coldplay. 2000. "Yellow." https://www.google.com/search?q=lyrics+yellow&rlz=1C1SQ JL_enUS886US886&oq=lyrics+yellow&aqs=chrome.0.0l8.2867j0j8&sourceid=chrome&ie=UTF-8. Coldplay and K. Nelson.

Diamond, D. M., A. M. Campbell, C. R. Park, J. Halonen, and P. R. Zoladz. 2007. "The temporal dynamics model of emotional memory processing: a synthesis on the neurobiological basis of stress-induced amnesia, flashbulb and traumatic memories, and the Yerkes-Dodson law." *Neural Plasticity*.

Hedstrom, J. 1991. "A note on eye movements and relaxation." *Journal of Behavior Therapy and Experimental Psychiatry* 22 (1): 37–38.

Jordan, J. V. 2018. *Relational-Cultural Therapy*, 2nd ed. American Psychological Association: Washington, DC.

Kip, K. E., L. Rosenzweig, D. F. Hernandez, A. Shuman, K. L. Sullivan, C. J. Long, ... and F. M. Sahebzamani. 2013. "Randomized controlled trial of accelerated resolution therapy (ART) for symptoms of combat-related post-traumatic stress disorder (PTSD)." *Military Medicine* 178 (12): 1298–1309.

Kip, K. E., A. Shuman, D. F. Hernandez, D. M. Diamond, and L. Rosenzweig. 2014. "Case report and theoretical description of Accelerated Resolution Therapy (ART) for military-related post-traumatic stress disorder." *Military Medicine* 179 (1): 31–37.

Kip, K. E., C. Tofthagen, R. F. D'Aoust, S. A. Girling, Y. Harper, and L. Rosenzweig. 2016. "Pilot study of Accelerated Resolution Therapy for treatment of chronic refractory neuropathic pain." *Alternative and Complementary Therapies* 22 (6): 243–50.

Kuhn, T. S. 2012. *The structure of scientific revolutions*. University of Chicago Press.

Strachan, A. L. 2016. "Memory Hackers: The Mysterious Nature of How We Remember" (*Nova*, season 43, episode 6). WGBH (television station, Boston, MA), Little Bay Pictures, LLC.

Rosenzweig, L. 2018. Advanced training workbook. Rosenzweig Center for Rapid Recovery.

Wolpe, J. 1969. "Subjective Units of Distress Scale." *The Practice of Behavior Therapy.*

Printed in the United States
by Baker & Taylor Publisher Services